DESCENT
OF
THE DOVE

DESCENT
OF
THE DOVE

CHANNELED BY
ANN VALENTIN and VIRGINIA ESSENE

 S.E.E. Publishing Company, Santa Clara, California USA

This book is manufactured in the United States of America.

Cover illustration: Sharon Nichols

ISBN #0-937147-03-6
Library of Congress Catalog Card Number: 88-090870

Spiritual Education Endeavors
Publishing Company
1556 Halford Avenue, #288
Santa Clara, CA 95051
United States of America

DEDICATION

This book is dedicated to God and the Great Rays who brought forth the many angelic souls who so magnificently demonstrate and fulfill their level of creation's promise.

It is also dedicated to the vast realm of angelic helpers, themselves, from the largest to the smallest, who in their unique spiritual form have respected and cared for us and our planet when humanity slept, unable to complete earth responsibilities.

From cherubim to seraphim, from messengers to the great archangels themselves, may our appreciation be known and our gratitude demonstrated by an enormous planetary awakening that resumes humanity's role.

This message is dedicated to and delivered for all the peacemakers on earth.

MAY OUR CONSCIOUSNESS FLOW TOGETHER
THROUGHOUT ETERNITY IN THAT
EVER-EXPANDING PURPOSE AND ACTION SET
FORTH BY GOD AND THE GREAT RAYS

ACKNOWLEDGMENTS

From Ann:

Commitment is a word often used to describe an individual's dedication to God, higher beings and humanity. With an appreciation beyond words, I thank Virginia for her demonstration of making a total commitment of herself, time and energies to pursue life and help bring peace on earth. The hours it has taken to bring forth this message are acknowledged with loving gratitude.

Personal thanks and appreciation to Micki Foster, who willingly assisted without complaint and was always loving.

Personal thanks to Elizabeth Flint for her total caring and support to us in blending her spiritual nature with the duties of SHARE/S.E.E. office and its work.

Also gratitude to Jo Denny and the office staff who, with loving hearts, kept things going while we were so frequently away.

Many thanks to my children, Lisa and David, for their loving support, help and understanding.

To our many friends who sensed the importance of The Dove's message, and have strengthened us by their loving support and caring . . . thank you!

From Virginia:

I want to personally thank each one who reads this book, who has read any of our other publications, and who has put any of the practical ideas into practice. It feels wonderful to see so many people genuinely involved with their own inner peace and planetary assistance these days! As we travel, we see much needed progress occurring quite rapidly. I particularly want to thank the many warm and loving folks who have arranged for our visits in and out of the United States, supported the work of the SHARE Foundation and S.E.E. Publishing Co., and become our spiritual family.

To those who are working on foreign language translations for <u>New Teachings</u> and our other publications, I am overjoyed by your dedication and service. May you receive a full measure of abundance for all you do.

Again, I am grateful to anyone who acts to resolve earth's problems. We are improving our situation only because of people like you whose intention is pure and who deeply care what happens. Know you are respected by those far beyond this place and will be guided to help the cause of peace even more as their spiritual plans are unveiled.

Archangel Uriel comes like a dove, yet I perceive a great power here. This one will not pull back from authority and responsibility, so I expect these next years to be very significant. Very significant!

Because of Ann's channeling ability, we are able to bring Uriel's message to you, and I extend deep appreciation for her work on this book. Her intention for peace and commitment to personal growth, as well, is very meaningful to me.

My sincere thanks to those of our office team and volunteers who have helped the SHARE Foundation and supported our S.E.E. Publishing Co. projects these past two years. Elizabeth is our angel-in-residence, assisted by Jo and others. I am truly grateful for their dedication.

However, you the reader are the backbone of planetary change, and you have my dearest gratitude for your personal courage and commitment and for persistent application of your own gifts and talents to this earth home we share.

Thank you for being who you are and for all the energy you give to make peace a reality and the planet's rehabilitation a certainty.

FOREWORD

Virginia's comments:

Through commitment and perseverance, Ann and I are co-producing the fourth book in our spiritual message series . . . this time from a wonderful (and new to us) being called Archangel Uriel. This book rounds out the spiritual overview we are assured is necessary to provide an understanding for present day life on earth in this Time of Awakening.

Because the spiritual call to action is so urgent a message, all of the books have expressed that theme at some level. The hours in each day since November, 1984, when I visited the Holy Land for the first time, have been fast-paced and often exhausting with simultaneous demands of travel for lectures, seminars, soul readings, book channeling and publishing. As the first portion of our task of publishing spiritual information is now accomplished with this fourth book, I am genuinely grateful. We are told that by setting this context to help understand what is happening around the planet, a new material will arrive now containing helpful information in a more scientific and technological vein. However we will continue to share a steady update of all information given us about humanity's progress in the Time of Awakening.

As I look in retrospect over the events of the last few years, I perceive each of the books has called us to take *action* for peace and preservation of life. Each book's author has said it one way or another, so our work is obviously focused on that *action concept*. Wherever you are, we hope this message reminds you to assist in earth's and humanity's reclamation by *your* own peace efforts!

Ann's comments:

No longer can words of peaceful intention be stated without actions to support them. Civilizations have come and gone. Peacemakers have also come and gone. Leaders have sought to unite us for global peace. Each of us, in our hearts, knows that the planet is not peaceful. Therefore, this message is a clarion call to all of us on the planet, to every lifeform on it, to unite *now* for peace through unity.

These words are for you to consider. Let them travel through your awareness to that place of knowingness and acceptance.

CONTENTS

NOTE TO READERS

In God all things are genuinely ONE, so beings who come from high states of consciousness often express this by the language of "we," "us," and "ours"—rather than "I," "me," and "mine."

Consequently, when these high energies communicate with us on earth, "we" is frequently used, even though one distinctive energy may be communicating. Please be aware of this as you read Descent of the Dove, channeled to humanity by Uriel. There will be some occasions, however, when the word "I" is utilized.

Also, please understand that the use of "he" or "his" does not exclude the feminine "she" and "hers." These spiritual beings and rays are androgynous. We ask you to accept the English language limitation in this matter as we say "he" or "his," and extend it to mean both female and male. There is no lessening of the female quality or nature intended!

Chapter I

Uriel

I, Archangel Uriel (Yur-ee-el), am here to speak to earth now as the angelic harbinger of peace. I have been asked by the highest of spiritual beings to help you awaken the beautiful expression of love and wisdom you were created to be while living in physical flesh.

You may symbolize me as a dove, yet in fact I am actually a 20-foot energy beam of pure white light with silver and gold radiance. Since earth's inhabitants know little about angels that is not distorted, I will explain some basic concepts about them, particularly who I am and why I bring my energies to assist you for these next several years.

Just as you have your earthly leaders and their assistants, we angels of the Light, created near the beginning of all existence as energy beams, had our levels of authority, of power, measured out into various sizes and capacities by the Great Rays. Your myths, legends and spiritual materials all acknowledge our existence, yet we observe that words such as cherubim, seraphim and archangel are difficult for you to truly comprehend. Because your consciousness is rapidly increasing, it is now important that you know us better, yet I am limited because you cannot receive tele- pathically. Hopefully these words will be of some value, even so.

How I became an archangel (as you call it) invokes memories within my intelligence, for I, too, have memory banks. Archangel is the title meaning an Illuminator or Radiant One who has achieved great responsibility. My existence began in the realm of "no-time," an existence without any measurement of longevity. Although I was created near the beginning of creation, I was not always an archangel or a being of importance. This was an achievement earned through my acceptance of universal responsibility with dependable, consistent results.

I have intelligence and feelings, yet my feelings are *soul feelings* and not on the human emotional level. Because of your body you have *emotions* that relate to what you call the five senses. I am a being without a physical body and those five physically related senses, so I cannot say that I have emotions. Nonetheless, I am capable of compassion and deep concern for life and have been involved with many projects in this universe concerning development of innumerable physical lifeforms. Soul feeling based on reverence for God is the primary quality we angels have in common with humanity.

Throughout the civilizations that have existed on your lands, there have been stories, legends, tales and prophecies of great ones who would come to "save" the population. These great ones, or saviors, would generally be either spiritual beings encased in human form or another God-creation called angels. You may be wondering how angels have the power to save, so let me begin by clarifying what the angelic kingdom is.

You are aware that God is an energy source whose intention to create by thought and will is the absolute beginning of everything. Yet you may not realize that this First Source did not itself directly create everything that exists, although it always provided the *energy* for all existence and manifestations.

In the beginning God created from itself two great rays of energy to continue the process of creating. These twin rays of energy were very powerful. They were over a mile long and half-mile wide, made up of pure God quality. One ray was golden in ambience and the other silver. Initially they did everything together. Later, the silver one was more dominate as a creative extension of its parent source, while the gold placed more attention on guiding and holding the created physical lifeforms in harmonious relationship.

To assist in further creative endeavors, the Silver Ray made "living" rays or energies from itself. The first of these 24 creations became what is known as the Elohim, or the Ancient Ones, who keep the omniversal records of all there is and has been. Created next were huge, colored sub-rays that you recognize as each of the rainbow hues. Then we of the angelic form were "born." We are a different expression of energy and intention than you are, and we precede you spiritual energies called souls. Your souls came later in creation's development.

Does the word angel invoke a feeling of intimacy within you? Many of you will say "yes" because you have read about us, and a few have clairvoyantly seen us. For some others, however, you actually retain an experience of a radiant archangel vibrating within a bluish light, telling you about a novel project on a new planet and asking if you would volunteer to go there as part of a spiritual scientific expedition. That was the Archangel Michael. For most of the original souls who volunteered to come to this planet, before you had physical bodies, it was Archangel Michael who you knew and loved. Gabriel, Raphael and I (plus two others not commonly known) came into earth's history later.

3

Angels, then, are specific beings created for specific purposes to support the Great Rays in the many universes. You are to understand that an angel judges you not! It *does not care* what lifeform you are, what physical dimension, age, skin color or even which planet you are resident upon. To an angel you are a being of God, and that is all that matters! You are a being of God because you were created *within* God's cosmic energy *by* the Great Rays using focused creative power also provided by the One Parent.

Archangels, of which I am one, have *very* specific duties or tasks to perform. Because we have earned the title of archangel, we are *responsible* for the outcome of any project assigned to us. Therefore, Michael and the other archangels are concerned for your welfare, as I am, but it currently is I who have been assigned the task of influencing the planet for a change of consciousness to peaceful existence.

At the directive of Silver Ray, I am "The Dove" to descend now and oversee the project for peace on earth. I am not here to tell humanity that all is well on earth. It is not! But because you, and millions like you, have prayed for peace, I am here to aid you by using the amplifying powers of God's twin offspring rays. *I will support all those who practice peace and compassion* because it is the time for a quickly evolving change to peaceful behavior on earth. This will involve supportive changes for each one of you as these powerful incoming energies blanket the planet. We bring you toward peaceful living, which should bring immense joy, since we are responding to your personal planetary needs.

The appropriate response to those of us carrying out the divine plan should be appreciation and cooperation because change can be a positive action. Since birth you have gone through many, many changes, for that is the way of life. Everything on your planet changes; nothing remains static in the universe. Accept this and cooperate with these new vibrations to quickly grow and attain self-mastery. That is their main purpose and function. Relinquish inappropriate and violent attitudes, and you will easily utilize these intensified energies. Only those who resist these increased peaceful vibrations will be uncomfortable and create difficulties for themselves. Then use our energy gift for noble or positive purposes only. And rejoice! Yes, rejoice! For the next two years will be so exciting that you will not have time to worry over unimportant things.

As this Time of Awakening continues with its fast-paced energy vibrations, many of you will feel the need and excitement of prioritizing your lives for personal peace and planetary survival. This Time of Awakening is one of the most unusual periods ever experienced on your planet. Never before has the very air or atmosphere seemed to crackle with these spiritual vibrations and energies everywhere. This high vibration is the current sensation of your life.

Because my mission is *urgent*, let me share my goals and purposes.

You are human forms living on a small planet spinning in space. You believe you are separate from other planets, but all guardians of the planet, from the 4th to the 22nd dimension, watch you because of humanity's misuse of free will.

As The Dove I am a mighty one who will come forward now with great energy and force for your edification and enlightenment. I have been working elsewhere in the universe with power and knowledge held in abeyance by the Silver Ray until the proper time sequence for use on earth. That time is now since we have evidence indicating planetary awakening is in progress, and the thirst for knowledge and enlightenment is growing. Those who are eager and committed will gain far more than mere words can describe.

Before coming to you, I was located primarily in the western part of your universe. Looking upward beyond your North Star, I would be to the left or western region of the universe, far beyond that which your human eye can see naturally.

In our western region some of the planets and star clusters are not as fully developed as C-ton (earth). Yet, under our angelic tutelage, there is activity and advancement in the western region.

After various assignments there of helping lifeforms develop to a higher awareness, or greater perception of God, I look forward to our task here on earth. Each archangel has its own time period assigned to your planet, and this period is mine. Through the portals of time each angelic power has been used, or will be used, for specific purposes in healing humanity's dilemma.

As mentioned, Archangel Michael was the recruiter for the new planet or territory you call earth. He also has had the responsibility of watching over the soul volunteers, helping with their training program, and protecting them as needed and when possible.

Raphael has had to do with creativity and some education. His most important period and influence will come during the Time of Radiance when true creativity will spring forth into great fruition.

Gabriel has periodically been a special messenger of high importance. It is planned that in the last quarter of the Time of Radiance he will lead all peoples into the unity of continual peace, even as I am here now as the forerunner to Raphael and Gabriel, as your leader of this Time of Change.

I am your Warrior of Peace, using the positive power of the "warrior" to dissolve all negativity and war. Peace, unity and harmony will be established. Yet, even as a Warrior of Peace,

I descend like a dove with kindness, even gentleness, to those who participate willingly. I am strong but am strengthened even more by the accentuated energies of the Great Rays.

Some of you resonate with Archangel Michael's energy very intimately so that merely speaking or thinking his name causes your soul to vibrate faster. Your soul retains a distant echo that still remembers the original pale blue clouds around the surface of this formerly blue planet. That memory recalls that you were pioneers in bringing God-grown seeds of life and beauty to be established and expanded here. It tells you of the beauty, not only of the land itself, but of each plant and living form brought forth to its highest level of development. That memory tells you of the daily work you did where the group progressed rapidly, adding experiences to your memory bank of creative expression and intelligence...of new skills acquired and utilized in God's name.

That memory also tells you of a bright light piercing through earth's cloud bank that ultimately caused some loss of consciousness to your soul's remembrance of God. Here, your memory may block, or it could bring forth recollections of suffering and pain.

This "fall" in consciousness did happen. These events are part of the history of your planet. It is from that negative influence your planet now requires change, *release.* That is why I am here along with so many others. Archangel Michael's duty is nearly done, although his energy will still be evident during the next 22 years, at a lesser degree than before, fading into the background in preparation for responsibilities elsewhere.

It is now time for The Dove.

As mentioned, until my current task on earth began, I have been working to your west in another region of this universe. For approximately 6,000 years by your measurement I have

7

been overseeing planets whose soul members also came forth to work with growing things, again using the primary color of green mixed with yellow.

The plant life on these six other places is much larger than what you have on C-ton, and only three of these six planets have physically dense lifeforms anything like humans. Nonetheless, perhaps one day some of your inhabitants will visit Karbella, the most advanced planet of the three just cited.

Although I have mentioned earth's past and its relationship to the angelic realms, we want you to move away from past memories and into the present, which will allow an exciting future to develop.

All four of us, called by you Archangel Michael, Gabriel, Raphael and Uriel, have made ourselves known to humanity at different times in your history so you would be aware of us and have a belief in us already imprinted. This belief allows you a point of reference and gives credibility when we begin to talk with you in this current period of awakening. As explained, each archangel has had or will have a specific purpose or project with C-ton. This purpose doesn't require humanity's belief to be achieved; however, your belief will aid you, for the divine plan is now operant. We share it with you so you will have a context for understanding past events and for focusing on its present phase more powerfully.

As I have explained, archangel is a term used as a title of power by certain angels who have earned that designation by virtue of dedication, responsibility and reliability, the latter having utmost importance. You may be curious about the rest of our angelic realms and your relationship to them, so let me speak briefly about what you call cherubim and seraphim.

This archangel designation does not make us "better" than a cherubim or a seraphim angel. It merely carries the added factor of being held accountable for accomplishment of our projects.

A seraphim is a very powerful energy being that is designated as an angel and has never been in a human form. Seraphims are perhaps 10 to 12 feet high but can be expanded either by Silver Ray or through their own service record. When contacting humans, they can focus into a very low wattage for teaching purposes, primarily. I, myself, was originally a seraphim. They contact human forms, yes, and bring information to those in human form, but *never* take the form of a human. In other words, none of the original angelic realm has ever been born as human, and humans have never been or will be angels. It is an entirely separate lineage.

That is because each was created for its own unique function or purpose. We are of higher energies and cannot be translated down and born into physical form. Angels were designated as life energies to be useful to the Great Rays at the very beginning of creation. It would be hard for you to imagine how busy these Great Rays were, and are. They need many others to assist them.

There are around 600 of these beings called seraphim angels, whereas cherubim are in abundance. I could not even give you an approximate number on them. They are one or two grades above what you call the messenger angel, beings who are the communication force of the Great Rays. They are about half the size of a seraphim. Cherubim work with a definite project, or even a location, to influence it with harmony or caring. There may be a specific place that requires harmony, and these cherubim would be *assigned* to go there. They can just drop down, enter earth's vibration and be among humans to change the vibration of a certain place. These smaller angels are very loving and gentle in their created nature.

For instance, when any of your biblical characters of sainthood, or high teachers of non-Christian religions, appeared on earth, they would be allowed to bring cherubim angels with them. As few as six or as many as 240 would just drop in and be with them like their "team" or as friends, just as you would ask your earth friends to go somewhere. From their heavenly connections, a being could call on the cherubim for support, and the cherubim would go. I believe your Lord Jesus did this on occasion.

Now there is one term that needs to be corrected in your earth language. That is the term "guardian angel." This one is *not* from the angelic realm but is a helper or a guardian assigned from spiritual dimensions. These beings are not presently in the dense physical form but have existed in physical form previously and understand humanity's struggle firsthand. They have *chosen* to be with you to guide, instruct and teach. Though they may be invisible, to call them angels is not correct. *Spiritual guardian* would be accurate, or just use the term teacher or guide.

In the actual creation of angels, then, the lowest or beginning energy level is messenger angel. Directly above the messengers would be the cherubim and then above them, the seraphim. There is one other angelic form that has the same purpose as the seraphim, almost a twin, but it is more powerful. It is used very rarely now, and I do not know what you would call it in your language. The Great Rays created only 144 of these. Each one is so solidly committed in its purpose that it will absolutely not waver. It will stay where assigned within a certain area and not deviate. Perhaps you would call it a watching angel or an observer angel. Its purpose is to monitor everything in a certain area. Your word observer might come closest. Those mammals you call whales and dolphins are likened to its activity. They were created to communicate important data, and they swim to designated areas where they take in the necessary information. They do not judge the information but forward it back to us at defined locations in space near the great star SIRIUS.

So you could say we have messenger angels, cherubim, seraphim, observer angels, and archangels. Now, let me pause and entertain any questions you have.

V.   In angelic realms does a messenger angel get promoted to be a cherubim and then further advancement up to seraphim, and archangel?

U.   No. Messenger angels are just that. They have no built in capability of intellect or striving. Like your telephones they carry communications. That is their *only* task. They are slightly larger than a cherubim but have less light intensity and capacity.

V.   Then where does that intellectual ability actually begin? With the cherubim or seraphim?

U.   I would say the intellectual ingredient, as you think of it, is part of the design of seraphim. They have the ability to think, to use intellect. They have retention of experience and a form of discernment. From their ranks we became archangels with increased energy size and soul qualities to support the Great Rays for God's purposes. It is because of my experience in the universe with similar undertakings that I am now competent and knowledgeable for my present task with earth.

V.   Regarding earth relationships with angelic realms, could you explain when and how our concept of you with human form and wings began? And was that a deliberate motive on the part of the angelic realm?

U.   It began thousands of years ago when we wished to describe the energy field around us. If you would search the ancient writings as they were originally recorded, they

11

described a luminosity around the angel being but not wings. From what we have been able to perceive, the description of the luminosity has been depicted in more recent time periods as wings by people who were involved in illustration and graphic presentation of ideas. They probably took it upon themselves to picture something similar that had motion, and they used the familiar human form with wings.

V.   Do you wish to say anything more about the way humans might perceive angelic realms in this Time of Awakening?

U.   Yes. There will be more accurate sensing of our angelic energies. There will be some humans who will at first see tall, strong, masculine energies. A few others will see softer, feminine energies. In both cases, however, these energies are just a projection that will then dissolve into the real being of pure androgynous energy.

V.   Is there anything else that you would like to say about being an archangel as *you* particularly have experienced that role?

U.   For me it has not always been *easy* to get down into earth proximity with the low density of a lifeform such as a human. This is because coming into simultaneous contact with your emotions and your free will factor is unsettling. Your free will and reactive emotional state is impossible to describe, but I will liken it to ten currents going on at the same time in each human being. You are similar to an electrical energy ball that has all of these wires going in and out of it concurrently. Thus, it seems like you have a variety of electrical currents on the same wires at the same time. These negative and positive currents almost combat each other. This occurs because your are *analyzing* data received by the senses while at the same time you are making a decision with the brain, hence you are *receiving* and *sending* at the same time. It has been very difficult for you to be a noble and stable soul while inside a human body, yet you are evolving, be assured, and with our assistance universal changes are happening very fast.

V.   Are you saying that the beings on the planets in the western region of the universe do not have free will and all this electrical confusion?

U.   That is correct.

V.   So your work there has been a little less challenging than what you experience here?

U.   Yes. The reason that your planet has its uniqueness and this urgency in the present time period is because billions of you are out of emotional control. Your pattern has become potentially unstable. We are not able to just drop a packet of information on your planet and have it utilized intelligently. Many of you pick up the packet, look at it, then throw it away! Most discard it! So we bring it back to you and say: "Look at it again."

You throw it away and we bring it back and try to present it a different way, hoping for acceptance. This struggle that continually goes on is even more difficult now because the Silver Ray has determined we will *only* be here a fairly short length of time. Our support is not going to continue for all of your existence. We are under a mandate, and so is each earth soul. So we bring our information back in new ways! We seek to give you new perspectives and brighter, wiser, happier consciousness. We are doing everything we can to have you comprehend what life and reality actually are through our use of high energy vibrations.

Right now we are working with thought expressions. We are endeavoring to work with *thought* and physical manifestation to bring you into spiritual alignment. Yet as stated by all your teachers, you must learn that *everybody* is responsible for his or her own energy uses, thought creations, and so on. There is not anyone who can speak for another soul or its personality's expression. Neither are you evaluated by others' levels of competence or commitment. Be assured that all of you will be known by your own application of willingness.

That is how I have attained my status. By proving reliable in each project that I have undertaken, I have earned my *merits*, so to speak, just as you do on your planet. Each positive experience that I create and complete gives a brighter, stronger illumination of my energy body or field. Each of us called as a lord or archangel have this power. We become amplified by each positive thing we accomplish. Now we are moving into a time period where I will have my particular energy at work on earth for just two to three years. I intend to fervently and intensely amplify my vibrations for *uniting all people for peace*. I am part of the power of the sorting out process. I am part of the *winds of change*.

In fact, I am working primarily with the wind element. We are not restricted to the use of only one element when we have a purpose to accomplish; we are allowed to use everything. There may be prior periods of time where you have been aware of an angel using water, earth, fire or wind. I have chosen wind because wind can change and bend shapes, turn things upside down! Because it moves I can use the elemental wind for *change*, and I will now use that wind to bring *sweeping* weather changes in and around you.

V.   Wind is not an actual, physical element by our earth definition is it? It is not like water, earth, fire or air would be.

U.   Yes, for air relates to wind, and wind relates to air. Wind is part of the movement within the cycle of your planet's sphere. You cannot fully perceive this until you

14

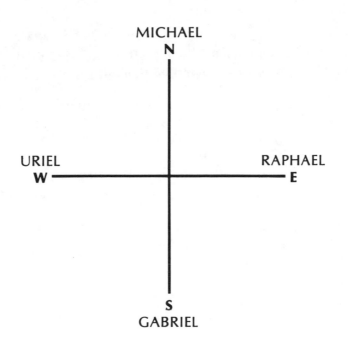

MICHAEL
N

URIEL   RAPHAEL
W ————————————————— E

S
GABRIEL

remove yourself from your planet and see from afar the
cycles and channels of wind that affect the weather around
your planet like an envelope.

    V.   Thank you. Could you clarify the "air" creativity
that you have said Raphael uses? Is this the same or
different than the air that you are discussing here as wind?

    U.   Refer to the diagram. Notice that Michael is to the
north. Raphael is to the east. Gabriel is to the south in this
12th universe, and I am to the west. I am saying that
Raphael is not forcefully energized on you at this time. He
has moved to the "wings," where I have formerly been in
regards to your planet. The present plan is for Raphael's
creativity to start in as a wave of thought and positive ideas

approximately 12 years hence. There will be certain individuals who will be selected to receive his pinpoints of
creative expression as they come across space. They will
take this energy and spiral it upward even though the
creativity will come in on a horizontal or linear mode. This
creativity will focus on giving the human being positive
ideas for a fuller potential of the entire species and will not
be for destructive purposes.

V.   Will these be scientific and technological ideas?
Or are you speaking more of the artistic and intuitive
aspects?

U.   It will be in all endeavors. All aspects that come
under the heading of creativity will be involved, such as
true science, governance, health and medicine, technological aids, music, art, food and agriculture. Everything
that improves humanity's thought process for manifesting
heaven on earth will be involved.

V.   Are any of you working with the physical lifeforms from beyond our planet called space brothers in any
of that dissemination?

U.   The possible angelic use of the space broth-
erhoods registers from only 2% to a possible high of 7%.
Not much information is going to come through them nor
for very long. Their technological contact is going to be a
"sweep." They will work with you very quickly, give
certain useful information and then leave. They will not
stop long, colonize, or remove your physical bodies to
safety. This plan would be too cumbersome and not allow
you completion of your caretaker's role on the planet's
surface.

Raphael will continue to work with advancing the intelligence of human beings for peaceful reasons and accomplishments. Because your souls agreed to be caretakers of

16

this planet, you deserve the opportunity to complete your soul goal with joy and satisfaction.

V.   Are you saying, then, that both you and Raphael are using air and not water?

U.   Correct. Water will not be used, although the planet is primarily water and *you* are water! Water certainly is the vitality base of your planet. In that sense anything that happens regarding the physicalness of the planet will eventually involve water because wind currents affect the oceans and, indirectly, the weather. These can and will affect earth changes of some kind.

Michael has been, and will be, giving information to your planet, but his task here is nearly done. He has been especially active and focused on *strengthening* people to get involved in both personal and planetary change. Because humans are undisciplined and use free will improperly, this plan hasn't really worked, and he will start to move back soon and progress to other tasks. He will still be very active for another year or so, however, while my own energies come to you amplified by the Great Rays.

It is I who am now charged with turning humanity around. I intend to lift your consciousness so you will peacefully look outward toward space, not to destroy it with your selfish and warlike concepts, but to truly revere God and your mission of peace *here*. The extended exploration, colonization or inhabitation of space will not be allowed until you have learned the ways of harmony and established peaceful natures.

Archangel Michael has brought encouragement and scientific information to humanity, but too few have been *positively* motivated. Therefore, *I* am going to awaken the sleeping ones with more wind energies. This will not have to be unpleasant. There may be times when the resisters will totter back and forth and perhaps fall down. We will pick you up, however, and strengthen you with heaven's combined energy. This is the Time of Change. We have heard your prayers and, as previously stated, we have tried different plans hoping to assist your required transformation of consciousness without a major intervention.

Now we are going to impress each individual's energy field until you make a choice one way or the other. I intend to elicit a final decision from humanity regarding peace on earth. Hopefully all will choose a move to unity. Be assured we are not going to let you go on and on just thinking about peace yet doing nothing positive. We are here to divide, to glean, to harvest, even as your holy books have described that process.

V.   What is the separation time everyone refers to?

U.   It is well that you should ponder this question. The separation refers to, and is considered by us to be, a sorting out of souls who are so engrossed in the personal part of being human that their reverence for God and bringing peace on earth has become a "distant" concern. It has become that "someday" factor in their existence. We note that many incarnated ones state that *when* certain conditions are right in their physical world *then* they will give attention to God and the issues of peace and planetary concern. The important time is *now* because sequential events make it necessary for humanity to help their physical planet immediately. Somehow the word *separating* bothers people because it implies failure. Please remember you are all in school, and evaluation is part of that process. The evaluation relates to fulfillment of soul commitment. That is the gauge and measure for this present life period. It does not mean you cannot repeat the course again. The division does not need to be permanent.

V.   What is Gabriel's responsibility in all of this?

18

U.   Gabriel will also bring forward information to certain individuals. Essentially it will be conversation to motivate and unite humanity in peace and to support our message that ultimately came from God through the Gold and Silver Rays. Gabriel may then withdraw temporarily to do other things while getting ready for a later combined energy surge and joint participation with me.

Again we speak of *probabilities*. He will be there at a specific time period when he will be needed to bring vital messages. He is not called a herald by you of earth for nothing. Periodically he will come in and support what I am saying so that there will be confirmation of information. He will not be a world-wide channeler to your species right now, however.

As you see, none of us angels have had anything to do with the scientific creation of your soul. We are not capable of this. You are already an evolving, if presently stagnant, creation which needs to awaken. We work primarily with thought energy to aid your own soul's remembrance, helping you become *aware* of the carbon and hydrogen elements in you and all things on the planet. *While these elements aren't our creation, it is our responsibility to have humanity stop misusing hydrogen and other elemental building blocks of what you call space, and return to reverence for God above all else.*

Please do not misuse God's energy elements, and please do not bring on this planet the potential nuclear, atomic and explosive fires that could come from your destructive devices and weapons. Rather, use energy to fire your knowledge of self, of the planet's needs, and then plan actions for love and caring. Because you are capable of turning an idea within you into a burning *fire* of outward action, we will all support this type of fire vitality.

As your awareness feeds and grows, like a fire being fanned, you will want to express that energy. Accept these fires of thought, these fires of passion within the heart, to motivate you. Let them move you out into that sphere of applied peace. With our caring, use the inspirational fire of our high energy vibrations for their intended purpose, and you will know cosmic reality.

V.   Could you explain why the names of your archangels, in our English language at least, all end in the letters el, such as Uriel, Gabriel and so on? What does that signify?

U.   It signifies a connection with the Elohim and the very early time period of creation when we were brought into existence. Use it to mean early lifeform, early existence, or near the beginning.

V.   Jesus has mentioned there are more than four archangels. Are any of them going to help us?

U.   Yes, there are 240 in the hugeness of this universe, with six in your immediate area. Only four are actually designated for your cosmic quadrant *since you have chosen only four directions.* You of earth have somehow divided your planet and space up into four sectors, so we are utilizing your present definition and process to see if we can get that conceptualization to work.

We four archangels are the most powerful now designated for this period on earth. However, there are other angels like ourselves who have earned high levels of esteem, power and authority, and are also helping you. They will not come in and say "I am archangel so and so," because most humans do not know their names. Just as I am not well-known, there are others you are not fully aware of.

20

V.   Did these original 240 beings all earn their titles of responsibility in the "early times" or were they added later?

U.   In the very beginning we were only six.

V.   Who were the other two?

U.   I must see how to give you the names using your earth plane language sounds. One moment please. I will given you a sound and you can put a spelling to it. (Sounded like Lekiel and Clariel, but this is only approximate.)

Although you have legends using the number 12, this is inaccurate regarding archangels on your planet. There were only six; however, we were busy moving about in many places and may have seemed like a larger group. When first contacting earth life we were not always always definite in our individual presentation of ourselves, so earth people might have thought we were two when we were only one. Since your universe and planetary area work with the number 12 you tend to expect that repetitive continuity. Nonetheless, we were *six*.

V.   Could you comment further upon angels, especially the devas and our relationship to them?

U.   Happily so, but there is a great deal to relay, so I prefer to continue in the next commentary.

V.   Agreed.

And now, citizens of earth, I must take my leave. Know our angelic power comes in caring concern but must also uproot any blockages that would prevent a soul from achieving its service purpose or goal.

Until we meet again, I send you compassion, wisdom and peace in the name of God and the Great Rays.

Archangel Uriel

Chapter II

Angels

Because angels have never been incarnated in a body and are pure energy fields, there may be imperfect recognition of what type of angelic being you have reached or that has reached down to you. Angels are not in your lower density energy levels such as 3rd, 4th or 5th. They are at a frequency totally related to light, which is beyond dimension five. However, your soul, even though it is small now, has recollections of ancient contacts with these angelic radiant beings. With a luminosity that brightens an entire room or area, angels dazzle your awareness with their pure sparkle and effervescence of cosmic energy. Truly you are seeing within that sparkle a form of atomic energy close to the vitality of existence. This vitality of God energy is so pure it fairly crackles.

As for knowing which classification of angelic being you are in contact with, it is necessary that you first question if it is of the pure and holy God consciousness, strange as this may seem. This question must be your very first! Then ask the purpose of its visit and ask it to give you a name. Most angels have names, or they will give you a number. All will tell you their classification and purpose, which is important information. To be in contact with an angel who does not give you a classification such as *archangel, cherubim, seraphim, observer,* or *messenger* opens you to the possibility of deception. Please follow this request and ask for identification from any non-physical being.

All messages from any angel in our realm are charged to move you toward personal participation in the Time of Awakening! Using your own soul/personality discernment, you are to be thoughtful when listening to any channeled information. Use spiritual discernment to determine the quality of any information received during this Time of Awakening, for you are experiencing an unusual planet-wide event. We are opening up memory banks within all souls while they still exist within time and physical flesh.

The veil that has been upon you for eons is now being penetrated so you can experience higher consciousness. We are concerned that, as you begin to see and hear us and other lifeforms, you may not know what to do with the new perception. We do not wish you to become confused. Most of you can enter into the light of this higher awareness safely and absorb it without mishap. A few careless humans have experienced mental distortions, however, and we remind you it is important to follow the guidelines given. This 3rd plane of existence has its reality. Since you live here physically you need to remain *grounded*. The soul works in conjunction with its physical body and needs both a physical body and emotional stability to complete its purpose in this life experience.

We angels and your spiritual teachers are here to give humanity a heightened state of consciousness or awareness, improved perception, and a reminder of your soul origin and current planetary responsibility. We come to assist, encourage and inspire. We honor your true essence and are here to serve in humanity's return to peace as is required by the Great Rays.

There are some teachings on the planet that say you are not adequate to the challenge ahead, which is certainly an invalid thought. You are absolutely capable but must be willing. Some teachings suggest that angels are bringing you back part of your soul or returning to claim the bodies that you now have, because a part of you was originally angelic. This idea is not true. We are here to expand your soul consciousness.

Let me be very precise in my comments. Angels and humans do not intermingle. Your soul did diminish from its larger seven-foot size, and the small portion now contained within your present physical structure is all there is. None of it exists elsewhere; it is presently inside your body at full size. You will not be increasing the soul's *size* because of our relationship with you, although you can improve its glow or radiance. Your soul will increase in brightness as you become a conscious servant of the light and help to heal planetary problems. I repeat for emphasis: Your soul energy is all in one piece and in one place—here, now.

Because you sense that diminished soul size, there may be a deep longing to be something more. Our role in your life is to guide you into higher consciousness, which is a different thing than soul size. If it were otherwise, we could not educate you for graduation to higher dimensions after your lifetime's accomplishments.

What your soul can reclaim, then, is its ability to reach a higher state of consciousness through personality cleansing, and it is this aspect you will use to solve the problems humanity has created on earth. The highest level or truest understanding of the Time of Awakening is realization that you will be changing lower perceptions and limited patterns into freer, higher ones. Belief is changeable within the thought process. Enlightenment begins with this step.

I truly hope it is clear that angels are not the same group of beings who have physical lifeforms and travel within their starcraft. Those on the starcrafts, called by us inter-galactic travellers and by you extraterrestrials, are working primarily with technological assistance and data.

Our spiritual purpose is revering God and helping others do the same. Your own reverence, awareness and spiritual understanding can be accelerated back to a more connected relationship with Universal Mind, which is all-knowingness or a superior consciousness compared to earth's. Since you have several definitions of consciousness on your planet, may I clarify how we define it?

Consciousness is the collective total thought of all that has emanated from the omniverse since its beginning. Consciousness is awareness of the full historical record of all intelligence that has existed. On your earth the consciousness is mostly your local planetary intelligence. This intelligence holds all life information that has ever existed whether from human, animal, plant, or mineral.

Anything within its unified local perimeter that can be known from those aforementioned sources is called *intra-dimensional*. Yet there is the ability to go far beyond this local planet's knowledge to the 12th Universe's consciousness. As you would surmise, this is the massive intelligence from all of the planets, stars and any created matter that is within this particular universe itself.

Beyond your universe lies an even higher accumulation of Universal Mind knowledge that is omniversal, and finally the all-encompassing cosmic energy, or God energy. This is all-knowing, meaning that it is able to transmit information as well as receive it. It is truly the container for all that is now, ever has been, or will be.

You cannot reach God consciousness yet, but other levels are available and will open up even further opportunities as you progress because you are working with what we will term electro-magnetics (just to simplify). You utilize the combined positive and negative aspects that make for movement of current, because God energy contains this electro-magnetic energy in a highly concentrated form. Within God's qualities is a higher energy level for which you currently have no explanation, and contained within this higher level of non-descriptive energy is what we have labeled, for your understanding, electro-magnetic energy.

The energy that emanates from God, called cosmic energy, contains electro-magnetic energy. Hence all that exists is able to move through cosmic energy while utilizing its electrical field to relate to the electrical impulses of the electro-magnetic field. Consciousness is not the electro-magnetic field. *Consciousness is merely thought, sound or expressed energy that is suspended or hanging within cosmic energy.* It has within it an electrical impulse drawing on the electrical energy within cosmic energy.

When you become attuned with energies, you are in fact becoming aligned or attuned to the energies that already exist. You are fine-tuning the frequency of your soul to a center point in a level of Universal Mind. Most created beings find this fact reassuring and informative. Within your 3rd dimensional physical density you somehow perceive this consciousness in levels, layers or bands; therefore, we use those terms in our discussions with you.

Our task is to help you exist intra-dimensionally with awareness of the physical capabilities of your body, brain, planet and all life here, yet also allow the soul its inter-dimensional communication beyond the physical body and planet.

27

Because this higher consciousness, or inter-dimensionality, is not far away and just takes willingness to attune to it, we recommend you relax into its healing presence through the inner stillness. You already go beyond earth consciousness when you are asleep or in some dreaming states. Then, you merely remove your awareness from the physicalness of the body and allow your soul to go beyond the physical body confines.

In inter-dimensional contact with the angelic realm, for instance, you are quite capable of learning that angels have levels of qualifications and service intentions. As mentioned, any being not in a physical body should be required to identify itself and clarify why it is with you. You must consciously ask it to do this, however. It is not usual for angelic beings to merely come and acquaint themselves or associate with an earth being without specific reason.

Because your planet is currently in a state of urgent need, the entire quadrant of your universe is working to assist you. That is why we have established a protocol or process to identify ourselves so that you will not be confused as to whether contacts are angelic, your spiritual teachers, or "star people"—those from other created physical worlds.

Now you might be wondering, "How can I sort out the angelic realms from my spiritual teachers in the higher dimensions?" By way of reply, let me say that we angels will assist you just as your spiritual ones do. They have had bodies; we have not. Nonetheless, both sources are here to help you achieve Preservation of all Life—Peace on Earth. All your activities are to relate to that theme. You are to clearly understand that although we are bringing information to help supply you with right choices and possibilities, your spiritual dimension beings are your evaluators and adjudicators. We are helping them help you even as we aid you to awaken for peace.

Before the Silver Ray's intervention, they would have been your direct support system. Because of the Great Rays, energy vibrations have changed and intermingled like a great chorus or symphony with many parts involved together. Now the information we all bring can help you solve personal problems, and it can also relate to government, health, agricultural resources, ecology, religion—almost anything that will move you forward to stop violence and establish peace. The changes that are necessary on your planet will happen when you use your thought processes wisely. You are a thinking machine. Everything that you do goes through the thought process. Thought process is your personal key to joy, love, wisdom and change on your planet.

It is important that you understand that no angelic being is going to incarnate as a human. Neither are we "walk-ins." The few of what you are calling "walk-ins" have to do with a temporary assignment by an intelligent physical being from a planet or star cluster that is using a human body by *mutual agreement* to quickly accomplish a purpose. Such helpful action is not considered an incarnation, merely a temporary utilization of a human vehicle with permission. Without exception incarnation always incorporates or uses the birth process, since the birth process is the mode of beginning human life on your planet.

An angelic contact is for a specific purpose to bring about a particular sequence of events. It is not to glorify any individual energy. It only identifies itself to clarify intention, as I am doing. Descent or contact of any angelic being at this time on earth is to assist in the awakening process.

You can distinguish the difference between the angelic descent of one or more beings such as an archangel like

29

myself, the Christ consciousness (energies coming from the Gold Ray to the planet) versus cosmic energy which is God everywhere present, in this way.

The *Christ consciousness* is a constant energy that shines down on everyone on the planet. It is energy of one of the first two born of God. We call it the Gold Ray. It is not selective but comes for everyone to use. This Light has always been beaming on your plane to hold a constant reverence for God in humanity's consciousness. The Gold Ray is a massive influx of the harmonic authority and will of God. Many great teachers have used it to maintain God consciousness when visiting your planet, but it is here all the time. The one you call Lord Jesus used the Gold Ray.

Cosmic energy is the God vitality everywhere present to sustain all life throughout the omniverse and provide a womb for further growth expression. It is God unspecified just as the Gold and Silver Rays are God specified.

In earth's history as a planet, it was the Silver Ray from God that planned the planet's lifeforms and growth patterns. Even the specific soul energies you still have were energized from God through the Silver Ray. However, once life was created it went on to other activities, leaving the Gold Ray's influence to maintain reverence for God and universal peace. Now, due to extreme circumstances, the Silver Ray returns to bring the unification or blending of *intelligence with soul feeling* back into the forefront of planet earth life.

Since humanity's intellectual accomplishments are not, for the most part, heart-based, Silver Ray comes to arouse your true respect for the beauty and uniqueness of your physical body design, the beauty and uniqueness of the physical planet itself as necessary for earth life's continuation. It is this issue of appreciation and caretaking that Silver Ray addresses most fervently and that has brought my own assignment here now, as well.

A part of your body, called the third eye, is that all-knowing center point of reverence for God. It is where the spiritual and physical intelligence unite in intention and become as one unit working in harmony for Preservation of all Life—Peace on Earth. It is this awareness we hope you will immediately use to rehabilitate your planet. This point is sometimes referred to as your intuitive center or place of God knowing.

Because Silver Ray has created massive energy beams called the sub-rays who are also focused here as part of the restitution plan on earth, these seven individually colored beams of your rainbow spectrum are also present to aid, each having a master or coordinator to focus it. So you are being greatly influenced by forces generally unknown to you, and this will continue for several more years, depending on humanity's response. The indigo sub-ray is the one I will most likely be utilizing in days to come, since it relates to that third eye area just mentioned.

Intelligence and caring are here in the greatest cooperative venture your planet has ever experienced, souls of earth. Thus, to avoid total confusion you will need to refine and use your inbuilt spiritual discernment and soul knowingness, which you often call intuition. Humans have the capability of think-ing and questioning within the brain, as well as in the soul's wisdom. It is appropriate to use it all now while our great circle of vitality moves closer to inspire and lead you onward.

Within our present energy spiral you are able to have the energy moving up as well as down so that we can energize you and also receive information as to how well we are doing in humanity's enlightenment process. With God's cosmic

31

energy, the Great Rays, the sub-rays and their coordinators, as well as the spiritual dimensions and our angelic realms here on your planet, we intend to synchronize all efforts together to accomplish the Time of Awakening. You are in a dangerous circumstance. You have moved your planetary and human life expectancy to an endangered level. This is the major reason for our present concern and assistance.

Thus, this time period, whether you call it the Time of the Dove, the Time of Awakening, the Time of Spiritual Understanding or the Time of Peace, is a time of our concern for you. Our contact with you, and to you, is to emphasize this concern and to move each of you forward to work for your own planet's welfare, as well as to understand life beyond your own physical boundary. Tune into your soul energy so that you can once again connect with the highest possible conscious awareness while in the physical body.

Please be informed that I, Uriel, The Dove, will use many means to resolve your planetary difficulties and personal negative emotions, whether it be the wind and weather, technology, or other useful aspects. Changes for individuals, families, groups and for an entire planetary family, are coming. Use your common sense and common purpose to become aware of life's simplicity regardless of the complexities you have created. Without delay, manifest the beautiful new life, the heaven on earth, you seek.

As stated, our mammoth activities mean that change will be dramatic, not soft. It will not be subtle, and it will not take a long period of time. It may be unexpected, and it may seem forceful and intense. Many changes will occur, some with impact. Know your true soul vision can be attained because of these changes, and remember that change is a momentum set in motion by us with planning and deliberation.

All life will be involved and must participate. One day your planet's history books will describe this immense change and cleansing as the event by which you moved forward to the Time of Radiance. Yes, it is inevitable. You will be moved to make the conscious choice of participation, the commitment "for" or "against" peace. It is an historical event, this choice, and we wish each of you individual souls godspeed in all you do henceforth.

Now let me pause and answer your previous question about a special type of angel you call devas. I perceive you use that word to describe invisible energies assisting the plant kingdom on earth. These devas come from the angelic realm classification called *cherubim*. They have willingly worked with your physical planet to aid its beautification, harmony and preservation during these eons when your souls forgot their original purpose as caretakers. Some on earth have called this event "the fall."

The intention of these devas, then, is the welfare and well-being of the physical planet, particularly plant growth. They do not need to care for minerals which are solidified color energy forms and are not essential to the *breath process* of all life.

These devas or cherubim are not projections of your soul or some separate part of you living elsewhere in consciousness. These angels are not returning to complete your humanness and neither are they a second coming of consciousness. *The second coming of consciousness is taking place within you*, however, with our help.

Through the years you humans have placed these cherubim or devas into classifications such as elves, fairies, gnomes, nature spirits and whatever else that sparked playfulness in your imagination. You were expressing in these terms a deep inner knowing that something invisible was at work. Different cultures may have had greater sincerity and affection for them, but that never determined a cherubim's (deva's) level of service. I shall henceforth call devas by their true angelic name of cherubim.

A cherubim accepts any project for a duration that is decided before the placement of its energy on the planet. This duration can either be days, weeks, or years in your time measurement. As mentioned, the reason these energies had to work with earth's plant growth is that humans have not fully redeveloped the caretaking skills relinquished and lost so long ago. These cherubim are utilizing those same skills that you still have within you and that you may once again utilize in the near future. Cherubim use the clouds, rain, wind, sun, fire and air to succeed in their projects and fulfill their responsibilities. They utilize these elements in harmonious relationship with the plants, using clouds when necessary, and so on. Each cherubim employs what is appropriate for the individual situation. There are no water cherubim, for example, or cherubim only for cloud use, sun use, and so forth. They use any or all of these.

Cherubim take care of the plants by communicating with them. This talking with the plant involves the *entire* item including the roots, stem, leaves and the environment around the plant. Just as your human body is a *total* package, with all of its parts involved in life's expression, and with its food intake affecting how you feel and act, it is the same with plants. What is fed to them affects how they feel and act. Like you, they need water to exist. Whether it is a salt water plant or a fresh water land plant, the condition of the water is vital to the health and growth. The cherubim can be considered your medical/technological caretakers of the plant kingdom. Through their instigation a person will often receive a thought suggestion or instructions about tending or assisting an ailing plant or area. A few gardeners and agriculturists are especially tuned into this type of receptivity. You say they have "green thumbs."

Nature spirits are the same as cherubim. Although they appear to be younger or older as they relate to an area with an extra buoyancy and joy, you are seeing them as you want to see them in your thoughts. As you relate and focus on a certain place with your thoughts and senses you will see the nature spirit with the combined awareness of these things.

Early on, when you true lifeforms first arrived for your participation on planet C-ton, it was understood that you would be working with the botanical aspect of the sphere. As you were fully tuned into and communicating with intelligence around the planet itself, you utilized the consciousness placed there by the Design Committee of Creation. This consciousness contained complete information about all forms of existence. As you original true lifeforms each worked with an item, you were able to directly tune into both the botanical item and also its related data as registered in planetary consciousness.

For example, if working with a plant called oleander, the true lifeform would *talk* to the plant and also obtain all the information about that particular type of plant from the data library available in the consciousness around the planet. Remember that those original beings were still in direct contact with the 4th and higher dimensions so it was an ordinary procedure for this to occur.

The initial design for each plant or growing thing came from the Design Committee of Creation, incidentally, and not from the cherubim. Cherubim are not creators. No angel is.

As mentioned, the intention of these cherubim is to enhance the given area where they are working and demonstrate the interrelationship of their energy with the plant growth of your earth environment. It becomes an educational relationship demonstrating the potential of the plant kingdom, as you call it, and clarifying the ways plants assist you in the continuance of your oxygen supply for life breath and the enhancement of earth's beauty.

Each plant has the potential of being a food, a healing substance, a purifier of air and water or of retaining air and water for other lifeforms. Part of the original agreement with the true lifeform souls placed on this planet was that they would work with its plant growth until one million varieties were completed. Prior to your full responsibility of soul dominion on the surface, all plants existed in a state of preparation for future use by all life such as animals, and later on, humans. Through the expansion of the fear factor in the original caretakers' intelligence, they began to distance themselves from their project, and angels were needed to assist. Particularly it was the cherubim who saw the needs of both the physical planet and its plant growth and volunteered to be involved in the temporary caretaking.

These cherubim angels, about 120 in the first group, joyfully interacted with the surface of your beautiful planet and its enormous potential for extraordinary glorification. As the true life beings perceived that they had received assistance from the cherubim, there was cooperation. However, through eons of time since then there has been a further lessening of the caretaking role by these original true lifeforms and their subsequent *human* (physical fleshed) family. In your recent times humans have abdicated full responsibility of nearly all caretaking work to our angelic cherubim. In one way this has been acceptable as a temporary measure, but during this Time of Awakening with its incumbent changes, this situation will no longer be acceptable. I will speak more about this later on.

Now humans perceive these cherubim angels as either very small or very large, again because of limited perception. Your perception is a combination of the size of the angel itself plus the energized perimeter of the items in the physical location. For instance, some plants are large, some small; trees can be tiny or gigantic. In identical fashion each forested mountain has a certain height and width. Since most humans cannot see or feel the background energy of the solid thing in relationship to the angel's size, you are quite often confused about what you have perceived. Thus, if you are looking at plants 24 inches high versus others that are six inches high, the angel's size will seem to be in a comparable ratio.

Because the angel can change its size, what you see may not be its actual size at all even before it joins with the different physical form sizes it serves. I attempt to clarify this topic and resolve your confusion regarding angels so your ability to understand them will be enhanced. In human history some of you may remember frolicking as well as working with cherubim for the continuation of life on this planet. Because we may return the responsibility of earth caretaking to humans again, you will understandably come to know angels again, my friends.

Now the cherubim who have helped your planet survive usually stay in any given area for 50, 100 or 200 years. It depends on the angel's desire to be there and its personal development in using the surrounding plant material. In other words, any area that may have had 150 years of angelic development does not necessarily mean that it has had the *same* angelic energy for those 150 years. There may have been a "change of crew" within those years. As you, a human individual, become more aware of your soul's purpose in serving your environment, and you begin to participate in the

37

care of these physical things, the need for these angelic assistants will diminish and ultimately cease.

Perhaps you are wondering if the plant growth on your planet would continue to survive without these angelic helpers or your own assistance. My answer is emphatically *NO*. The plants would *not* survive! There would be a length of time where they would survive due to momentum within the plant and the energy within the canopy around your planet. Eventually, however, all plant life would cease because it was designed to interrelate with human and animal existence. Since animals cannot be caretakers and the plant kingdom is designed to be part of sustaining earth life, you humans would have dominion. (Your religious scriptures explain this fact yet you do not fully understand them.)

Is it clear to you that the true balance of existence would be so distorted that eventually all living forms would cease to exist? Can you accept that the very source of all life, including your oxygen and your food chain, would be so imbalanced that physical life would end?

The purpose of what you call the plant kingdom is to provide a life support system. Plant life must be nurtured to fulfill its purpose and cycle of support to you. Otherwise, the life chain would cease to operate and exist, with obvious effect on all breathing things, including humans.

This danger is one of the primary reasons I have been sent. We want you to stop exploding hydrogen as it is an integral part of cosmic energy and relates to all created matter. Because every living thing has hydrogen within it, why would you explode hydrogen inside or above the earth, risking death and disaster? Will you allow a few madmen to use God's power without God's caring? Many humans understand this, yet the *majority* do not and must act quickly to change such dangerous activities.

Our angelic realms have been helping God's forces on your planet maintain life here in more ways than you have grasped. Now, as part of a divine plan of restitution and rehabilitation, our delegation must awaken you and assist humanity to resume its own original task of dominion.

Through this discussion I trust it is becoming evident that the energies, whether from the Great Rays or our angelic family, have not been used by humans for positive development. In your negative personality domination, also known as ego, you have put the responsibility of the caretaking function on us for your own survival instead of continuing or redeveloping your own participation. *This irresponsibility is not going to be continued.* It is absolutely *urgent* that you begin as individuals, and as planetary citizens, to care for the planet yourselves. Soul remembrance and understanding are being revived and recalled in each of you so that ultimately *the responsibility for the planet can be returned to you!*

You have the intelligence, technology and physical capabilities to care for it. Therefore, to avoid an emotional shock of one day waking up to find you have *all* the responsibility, begin this day to participate with your thoughts and actions in the care of the planet while we engage in this eventual changeover.

Pick up your plastic litter and non-biodegradable objects and create a usable solution to that type of waste. Avoid materials which cause heavy gases that stay in the atmosphere when they are burned.

Use fresh water sparingly. Your attempts at reconstituting water for human consumption must be strengthened and restudied. Also study the topography of the land to determine the natural flow of fresh water so you may use it wisely. And do not poison what you have! Learn about the *frequency* application of moisture that is the key factor of growth, and do not engage in wasteful watering. A plant has an innate capacity for measured intake and once that amount is reached, any further watering is wasted moisture. Just as when a glass if full, any additional liquid being poured into it becomes overflow or "waste." Learn how to deliver the exact amount required.

Planting of seeds for vegetables, grains, flowers, trees, shrubs, when done in conjunction with the moon's phases, will have faster germination and/or strength of the stem. All life on your planet is interrelated with the moon and its gravitational pull.

Your planet is a magnetized matter mass. It utilizes the *pull* of gravitational energy as the growth energy within is being *pushed* up by the energies inherent *in* the earth itself . . . and also *pulled* by the force of the moon with its effect on your planet. The moon is not there merely for reflective purpose and illumination during your so-called night. It has a functional relationship to your planet for the growth process. As you must know, it affects all water movement on the planet including the water contained within your own body.

As you begin, or continue, this study of growth, use the natural ingredients of the planet itself. Use your leaves for warmth of the roots, use branches to make shade to cool the roots and stalks of a plant or tree. Study the roots of plants that you call weeds to see how they hook themselves within the soil to allow air circulation there. Study the worms, bugs and all insects that are within the soil as they help the growth process.

Begin to *talk* to the plants and all growing things. Begin to *touch* the soil and the living growth, as many primitive or simple people have done. *As you feel the planet with your senses it will talk to you, tell you who you are and help you attain harmony with your environment.* The angels have already established contact with some humans who have learned these things and are modeling them for you. If you cannot contact us or the plants themselves, please learn from your human teachers. But *LEARN!*

This understanding of the moon and gravitational energy is the key of knowledge that our cherubim, or your "devas" use. By now you are aware that *all* matter contains electrical current. This current is influenced by the exterior environment, the generating of energy from the planet itself, and the activity within the atmosphere. This blending and weaving of energies is part of the intra-relationship and inter-relationship you have to *all* existence.

There is a vitality within water that is amplified by the influence of gravity and magnified by the pull of the moon. As you accept this as a scientific principle you can understand that change within matter is occurring all the time, even when you think that nothing is happening. The process of change is continual! *The entire process of change is intended to move the thing itself to its full potential.* This includes you of the human family.

It is important to be aware that *each human form, regardless of its official occupation, has the responsibility of being a caretaker for the planet itself.* All plants, whether they are food-bearing or not, are involved in your welfare as a life-support system on this planet. They are your planetary oxygen apparatus—a mammoth breathing machine. You need them. I could never stress this fact enough. In destroying plants and trees you are killing your life-support equipment for the soon-to-be 6 billion humans, and an even larger number of birds and animals.

Fortunately, the unfolding of your caretaking memories is occurring and some of your people have already created

41

model farms and gardens. Many of these farmers and gardeners who attend their work so busily and diligently—those who *love* the earth and planet itself—are primarily humans whose souls have the green Ray of Intention contained within them. They want to feel the beauty and vitality that emanates from the greenness of life on the planet. They want to help it continue. Yet, even if your soul ray is not green and you are involved with other activities, each of you must begin to accept the responsibility for taking care of this unusual planet. Your holy books call it the Garden of Eden. We call it the most beautiful place in the universe.

By virtue of the vast number of lives on your planet you must become mathematical and perceive that the need to work with plant growth is of *primary* importance. We will endeavor during the next two to three years to have you understand green growth underneath the seas, also. Again, some of your people have found the key to ocean foods and oxygenating plants. Please remember that the color green contains the vitality and life promoting qualities you need to survive. Your life-pattern substances relate to green on both land and sea.

Because of the high probability there could come a time where our cherubim would withdraw and leave you to your responsibility, I urge you to appreciate God's plan of interrelated existence now. Honor life with your soul, mind, heart and actions. We will not suddenly abandon you, yet consider what you would be faced with in the full responsibility of your own survival regarding the plant growth for food and the breathing process of life.

Silver Ray has set the stage for this possible transfer, as described, by putting a love awareness for the planet in the collective consciousness of your people since August, 1987. This assists in awakening your responsibility for self and regaining your dominion again as a true lifeform on this planet. The fact you have not been attending to your responsibility does not change your original contract for this, does it? I say this merely to make you cognizant that the life and circumstances on the planet ultimately reside with humanity as the individualized energy residing here.

Any being or lifeform that comes from another dimension into your plane of existence is merely here to assist you or to aid the planet itself. It is not here as a permanent energy to relieve you of your personal responsibility.

These cherubim angels presently on your lands are lovable and joyful, though equally serious in their tasks. Can you be the same? Will you now perceive these angels and accept that they are sending you their knowledge about growth? their happiness of being involved with the physical beauty of this planet?

We support your willingness to make this connection with any or all of us because within your soul, where your truth exists, you will more rapidly remember why you are here. The happiness that you receive or sense from your communication with any angelic being is part of that remembrance already deep within your soul. Rather than have these as mere isolated instances seek now to open your total awareness and perceive the beauty of this planet in its truest creation. Then your human family will be ready for whatever the Great Rays decide about this issue of planetary caretakership and dominion.

Know that as your helpers we will diligently assist God's original plan of creation to express its purity, wisdom and beauty wherever we are sent.

Our many ranks have served you of earth as teachers, gardeners and caregivers for a very long time, my cousins. Now we will be with you in ever-increasing devotion as you

43

awaken from a long sleep and return to complete your soul's yearning and satisfactions. By surrendering your amnesia to awakening love, once again you will be truly alive and functioning as part of the eternal and constant vision of our mutual Creator.

Each created energy form has a design of purposeful expression. We have ours in direct membership and service to those Great Rays, the first two born of God. You, also, have, in your form, been created to love God and serve in the vast dimension of cosmic expansion. As you acknowledge both your divine origin and functional responsibilities your soul will emote a symphonic sigh of life only hinted at in your slumbering experience of forgetfulness.

Welcome home, dear friends and members of God's family. By such messages you will remember and reign again as a resurrected and transformed light being of cosmic estate.

Take a moment's quietude to recall your soul's purpose and our mutual endeavor as I cease this language communication. Join our light with yours. Shine, created soul. Shine! In this unspoken bonding is your true reality reclaimed.

Chapter III

Soul

Because all life is energy, even we angels have souls, for souls are composed of *creative* energy from the Great Rays. Except for the first two born of God, the Great Rays, and the sub-rays, all energy beams could be considered as souls. The Great Rays do not consider themselves souls because they are umbilically extended from their parent and have that attachment even yet. They consider themselves both created and creative beings. They are energy forms in the truest sense since they emanate directly from God and are an arterial extension of God's primary vitality. We heard a small child call the Gold and Silver Rays "God's arms" though God has no physical body, of course; nor do these two Great Rays.

That God-magnificence and power amplification is the Great Rays' very nature, whereas our angelic realm and later the souls you have—are not directly linked to the Great Rays or God. We are individuated. We were given a singular mobile energy form by the Great Rays, greatly reduced in size and prowess.

A soul is a movable life essence of radiant energy that is so illuminated that it is perceived as light. The power and force of God from which all things ultimately emanate is considered unmovable itself. Nonetheless, it provides a steady outward flow of cosmic energy supplying a never-ending womb for the development and support of that which it creates via its first two birth expressions, the Great Rays. God is a self-sustaining, self-sufficient force of energy within itself that emanates two types of energy outward—*cosmic* energy to put things in and *creative* energy to materialize things that live in its cosmic womb.

Your soul energy beam is composed of God material and is designed for a particular purpose. It has intelligence, grace and memory. While your soul energy is the same composition as my own, and we are basically both a beam of energy, we are not God. Angel souls and human souls are distantly related but have different purposes by creative intention or birthright. On earth these days we hear you say, "I am God," to help you gain self-confidence. To say, "I am energy" or "I am light," would be more accurate. However, we understand your motive.

A created energy soul is not a mixture of masculine and feminine properties in equal balance, contrary to some earth beliefs. Of itself a soul has neither quality. You often misuse the term androgynous. To us androgynous means it is neither masculine nor feminine. While you exist on the 3rd and 4th dimensions, the soul has an accompanying information bank because your physical body has sensory capacity and a biologically identified sexual form. However, while your body is either feminine or masculine, the soul is neither.

I hope by now you perceive that there is in each created thing the ability to comprehend God, that supreme and awesome force *behind* and *in* all creation. Everything, at its own level, has this innate understanding.

Whether you look at a tree, a flower or yourself, you eventually must acknowledge some *unknown* factor as cause of its creation. Humans do not create the seeds containing life for themselves, animals, birds, plants and so on, but their soul knows who does . . . God and the allied parts of itself.

As an example, in analyzing the human body a doctor or scientist can comprehensively describe the functions of the human eye. They tell you how the eye works like a camera and how the picture gets to the brain. Here you should realize that the camera is similar to the eye and its brain memory banks, not the other way around.

As you scientifically analyze your physical body you are able to explain each part of it, able to understand why and how your fingers, hands and arms operate. However, the one part of the bodily life that cannot be reproduced independently is the ingredient that starts and maintains the life function—energy. Just as a fine automobile with all its appointments and styling cannot function without its battery or energy source, neither can your body. It is true that you are made in God's image because you are a continuing energy beam creation made from the same materials. Your physical body is not the image referred to in some religious interpretations, and any teaching that you are merely a physical body image of God is incorrect! Such beliefs limit human perception and our attempts to awaken you.

Does it seem logical that you would have an existence merely for a few years and then cease to exist? No, you continue to exist as a soul energy and are energized by the cosmic energy force whether in or out of the body. The soul continues yet has a purpose right here, right now. Then move courageously forward to fulfill that purpose of personal and planetary peace.

Your soul capabilities of telepathic communication, talking to animals, and soul-to-soul communication may have diminished through life experiences (incarnations); however, the abilities are still there even if lessened in power by lack of use. The day will come when unused parts of the brain will restore these functions once again.

Presently you have a soul and body with a functional brain. Your body cycles take you through birth, maturation, and eventual decline to death.

Through its senses the body learns skills and acquires its own information. Your soul *also* acquires information at the same time. It becomes selective in the retention or storing of the information, though, and does not remember and retain all experiences. Your brain cannot make this choice. It retains *all* thoughts and experiences. By comparison to your present technology, the brain is a super, super computer. It is capable of analyzing each situation and rendering the choice that it determines is an appropriate response. The brain is only a functional part of the body machine that starts to acquire information while still in the womb. *All* experiences are retained and directed out to certain categories for information filing. The five physical senses are important in the acquisition of this stored data.

The human body machine can use the electrical current contained in a specific electrical field located inside the skull's frontal area over the physical brain matter. You call this function intellect or intelligence. It is actually a sub-level of cosmic energy at a higher frequency of molecular activity than the rest of the electrical current used in and for the body's conscious and unconscious functions.

Briefly, then, the intellect is the analytical part of the brain that receives and gives information, yet becomes automated for certain common and repetitive functions through agreement with, or decision by, the soul. Automation such as picking up a pen, putting on clothing, and so on, can occur at any time during the life and for unlimited numbers of subjects.

Personality or ego are words you use to describe what is occurring within the intelligence field. It makes approximately 60% of the everyday decisions necessary to carry out ordinary human life functions. Only the soul's influence prevents a human from being a robot.

The soul is a compacted cosmic energy field in constant communication with this intelligence field; because it is at a higher discernment level than the intelligence field, the soul has dominion. The soul is the ultimate decision maker and must bear responsibility for the behavior of the entire unit except for automatic body responses like breathing and digestion.

As a monitor or scanner, the soul energy releases some choices to the intellect so it is not bothered with repetitive details. The intellect is never the ultimate decision-maker.

As the amount of information is increased, it is filed by category or subject in the information center (the brain). Further experience or a sensory event in the senses tell the brain what is going on; the brain tells the soul what is happening via the intelligence field.

Since so many of your daily or habitual activities are placed in the front of the brain's information center and labeled "frequent use or automatic," most humans live their lives unconsciously. This automatic thought process occurs at an incredibly accelerated rate.

I remind you of this because many times the soul becomes fascinated with the activities of the body and its senses and chooses to ignore its purpose in the life experience. Even a partial or temporary soul detour can cause later regret of serious magnitude.

The soul always knows, however, and can quickly recover its recollection of purpose and commitment!

All humans have either experienced this need to balance soul and intelligence cooperation or will be faced with it now. These high vibrational energies we bring are insisting on examination of and commitment to soul purpose. Truly it is the Time of Awakening!

While we are presently focusing on you earth souls, you may be sure that the humans on earth are not the only God-created souls that exist. Souls can inhabit many distant places. For example, some planets in your universe revolve so quickly that 24 of your hours would only be about six hours there. What would a soul experience in such an environment? Other planets revolve so slowly that there is no sense of movement at all. If a soul were there, what would it learn?

Another planet, called Meon II, located in the western region of your universe, has ensouled inhabitants approximately four feet tall who are wonderfully pleasant. You would say they smile all the time. They have no noses, only two eyes, a mouth and pin-point ears used as sound sensors. If your soul were embodied in flesh there, you would have no sun, only stars with three planets visible. Has your soul ever been on the surface of a planet where rocks have a luminosity that gives the planet a soft glow at all times? What would you learn about life on such a place, where the maximum lifeform population is just 12,000 beings?

The same type of lifeform I just described was used for your solar system's planet, Mars. Mars is actually Meon I. If you ever hear mention of any place called Meon, it refers to a lifeform design given above, which has a small planet size with limited, compacted mineral content.

So your soul visits are learning experiences, wherever you go and whatever the body-form composition is. Of course, each planet or star's lifeform is related to the substance of the planet or star where it resides. You presently have a body-soul container that has a denseness related to the basic carbon content of your earth. This has been a unique adaptation for your soul to allow its fuller participation with the planet itself and all things on it. Incidentally, you did not have to experience this lifeform, but chose it so your soul could understand such things as a tree more fully. Having chemical components of a thing as *part* of yourself gives you *insight* into it.

When a "body" was designed for you, after your soul size diminished, it was not intended that it become so heavy or dense. In fact, the original body design was almost a transparent form. Through later negative experiences a closer, tighter molecular modification developed. This unforeseen molecular modification affects the present functions of your soul container (the body), primarily in telepathic communication, true soul-to-soul awareness, and conscious travel to other dimensions. *However, your dense body has not changed the original purpose of your being here on this planet!!!* THAT PURPOSE IS TO EXPERIMENT WITH GROWTH OF TREES, PLANTS, ANIMALS, MINERALS—EVERY FORM OF LIFE—AND TO MAKE THIS SPHERE A GARDEN. You were volunteers for this task and agreed to your responsibilities. This cycle you are in now is the soul's requirement to complete that original soul contract.

Perhaps you will ask what difference does it make for you to know such information. Will it really make any difference to your welfare or bring you personal benefit?

The answer is yes only if you will comprehend, awaken and take action. By now you should be very familiar with the word *awakening* because the term has been used frequently these past two years and will continue for another two years, or more. This word *awaken* will continually pop up in conversation, lectures, songs, advertising, and other media presentations. This is the *Time of Awakening* when the personality and soul move into closer harmony, and the soul expands to its true spiritual awareness.

In the Time of Awakening, the *key* is personal soul responsibility as the basis for group awareness and participation. The expansion of this by each person, by each soul in this life experience, is mandated. There will be no ignoring it! You are either a conscious or unconscious participant. Our higher energy vibrations, something like electricity, are there in your atmosphere. Whether you believe it or not, each of you has a purpose for peace.

Not all soul purposes will be gigantic undertakings, but they will be action-oriented and related to peace and love. These purposes will be a blending of each individual's talents with others to create a tapestry of human caring. This tapestry will register the energy of each person as a magnificent colored thread in a cloth of peace that sparkles with the radiance of the rainbow.

Your soul can still exist along with your intelligence field and be you. Do not fear that you will lose your identity. This is not so! Rather, you will be enhanced as a soul and become more balanced. As your soul seeks and finds expression as a total God quality in matter, you will flourish and flower in joyous richness of energizing relationships and mutual cooperation.

Each of you will benefit individually and collectively from this experience. Artists will more easily capture beauty. The musicians among you will hear sound that is celestial, and all will hear more clearly the natural earth song of dancing wind, flowing waters and singing birds. Truly the sounds of the earth itself will be felt and heard by those who choose to listen.

But to ground this experience in everyday circumstances, there has to be practical application of this soul purpose principle.

Our recommendation, as so many before us have stated, is that each of you have a quiet time alone each day wherein you do the following:

1. Absolutely love or care for yourself. If you feel improvements are needed, attend to them. Make a genuine effort. If you have done harmful deeds, see the deeds, not you the person, as wrong, and seek to correct your conduct. In choosing to change, the opportunity for greater awareness can embrace you with sun-bright speed.

Each of you is responsible for your own deeds. You are within cause and effect circumstances in this life, although Lord Jesus has granted grace concerning all previous times. It does not matter what you call it—in this life your actions bring back an energy result or effect.

2. Learn to relate with other people on a more even basis. Have respect for each other. Judge less and listen more. Learn to truly communicate with each other! It is essential that truthful and caring relationships with all others be peacefully intended, developed and practiced.

Think of yourself as pure and whole and others the same. You cannot pretend at this! Your soul knows your truth, as do we.

Now kindly pause and consider what soul awareness is. Have you ever felt it?

When ...?

Where ...? Do you enjoy this broader more wondrous consciousness?

In the ensuing months you will be hearing more and more from me and from Archangel Gabriel about this consciousness. Archangel Michael will be here, too, but at a lower level of intensity. Archangel Raphael will appear to some, but with a gentleness, whereas I come to energize and vitalize you into action. We need you out of your complacency and disinterest (if any) and involved in cleaning and healing your planet, loving and caring for everything that lives. The theme for the Time of Awakening is now here for accomplishment!

The influence of The Dove is intense, stimulating and progressive. Fed by energies from the Great Rays, I will make an additional difference on your planet, along with help from many spiritual teachers of all beliefs, such as Jesus, whom you already know and love.

Since your soul energy has built within it responsibilities to life, to your planet, galaxy and universe, we belong to a mutual endeavor, a unified venture to resolve disunity and violence.

As each breath and each thought has the ability to change your consciousness, hear my message at all possible levels: body, emotions, mind and soul. Know I do not take my responsibility for this planet's well-being casually. Its welfare, your conduct and earth's relationship to the rest of existence all have my full attention. This necessarily involves change at many levels because *the universe is not static*. Earth's situation cannot remain static, either.

You are a living energy, and your body needs a place to live, does it not?

"Yes," you surely say, and whatever your nationality, that place is somewhere on the planet itself, which has been abused for too long. That which you have called Mother Earth keeps acquiring more and more abuse, but she may soon reach her maximum ability to absorb any further damage. *She must receive caring*. Harken to the needs of the planet. The planet has nurtured you. Nurture it.

54

Your very life cycles are being damaged by the constant destructive impulses to the planet's electro-magnetic field from nuclear and hydrogen explosions. You blindly play with an element of creation, hydrogen. Hydrogen is an ingredient for bringing life into manifestation, and you dare not misuse it without perilous consequences. Please heed my comments seriously! You cannot presume that ill effects will not occur.

Your abuse is changing major life patterns, and those changes mean deviation from a divine plan. To blindly tamper with atomic, nuclear and hydrogen elements is both foolish and evil. Unfortunately, results from such action are not always evident until a malfunction or negative reaction brings horrendous regret. But I shall not dwell on it further.

There has been an endeavor to use atomic and nuclear power for peaceful pursuits, that is, non-destructive intent such as medical purposes and transportation. If you continue to use nuclear power thusly, you will have to use a formula that neutralizes the waste product, so that destructiveness is not a by-product of the non-destructive use.

It is our intention that your planet, through your research technicians, will utilize the powerful energy of the sun, thereby not endangering any person, animal lifeform or the planet itself.

Now it is my spiritual commission and soul pledge to you that I come to energize this planet's consciousness to its maximum positive potential so you will be swimming in a pure and wondrous light. This light requires usage, however, and I fervently ask you to bathe in it, to dream and meditate in it, and, most vitally—to take action with it.

The light we bring removes fear and reinstates purposeful clarity to present issues. This light is soul sustaining. Use it for creative thinking, planning and cooperative advancement. This renaissance gift strengthens you with a heavenly resolve and magnificent intention. The blind in consciousness are offered spiritual sight. The over-intellectual and disdainful are offered compassion. The murderous can be filled with mercy and peace.

You are God's offspring with an ancient heritage to claim and universal law to practice. I have pledged our angelic support to the Great Rays and our Creator. We will not falter in fulfilling the reclamation of this planet's cosmic heritage. Then accept this light for new thinking, new actions, and forward movement into a peaceful 21st century.

I come to inspire a slumbering world and will reside in true partnership with all who will listen and care. You need not falter or fail with our divine strength and power around you. Come forward and achieve success. Truly, until time ends in a rush of conscious reality, we have a great providential work to accomplish.

But let me pause to see if there are questions.

V.   What is your experience of these Great Rays you speak about?

U.   My own experience with them and their creative process is that they are in a supreme place where they perceive all things and where their power and magnitude is unquestioned. We angels are designated to have certain occupations or projects to complete and we then go on to something else. The Great Rays are a distant all-knowing source of energy to us with very nearly the same respect as we give the Creator.

I have had the surprise awareness of the Gold or Silver Rays appearing near me at either announced or unannounced times, whereas my relationship to God is that the Creator is at a distant place and would never be physically near me.

56

V.   Even though you live in the sea of cosmic energy that keeps all creation alive, you feel no other direct relationship to God?

U.   Correct.

V.   Could you discuss the various sizes of souls in the angelic realms and give us some comparison between the smallest messenger angel to the cherubim, seraphim and archangel?

U.   Our size has to do with who we are. I am a soul of archangel size, about 20 feet high, as perceived by you on the earth plane. My width is changeable, depending on where I am and what the intensity of the presentation requires. Normal or usual would be a shaft about 18 inches wide with about eight inches depth. However I could compact myself to a half-inch in width, or expand up to 24 inches wide, if necessary. We angels usually appear as a shaft or column of light, but we can also appear as a bendable form. It depends on what impression we are trying to make. Sometimes the visual impact of us standing as a light force is necessary. Other times we may wish to bend and appear protective. It depends on the circumstances.

V.   Are you saying you have the capacity to take many guises?

U.   Yes, we can appear within the thought process of a human being as something else before you realize that it is an angelic form.

V.   Do you do this with all physical life forms, or are you speaking now of the ways you have to appear on earth due to our various historical writings about what angels are and do? For instance, in your western quadrant of the universe, do those inhabitants respond like we do?

U. We use that conceptualization with all created forms, so wherever we present ourselves the being can comprehend. We are, in our full amplification, very, very powerful energy beings. This adaptation or taking another form is only for a short period of time, however. It would be no more than six minutes at any given time; the minimum can be even 10 or 20 seconds in your perception.

We do not wish to fully adapt ourselves to any one situation permanently and lose our natural energy form which, if our power became diminished and diffused for extended periods of time, could occur. This is true for any angelic form. My own shaft can change to a smaller point of intensity if I wish to penetrate through any of the lower dimensions, such as your earth level.

If you saw me, my energy field would be rather like your soul—radiantly gold and silvery—but much larger. When we are working with a specific purpose, as I am now, an archangel may also draw on the appropriate colored sub-ray to present something to you for forcefulness; however, I am not currently using any of the individual rainbow rays to present myself.

V. Then you are not the being that Silver Ray has described in his book Cosmic Revelation as the one who would be coming to the planet on the indigo ray?

U. Yes, I am. And I will be utilizing that indigo ray toward the end of my earth responsibility. I am not here as a ray primarily. *I am here as a powerful angelic being, a spiritual force to change the world!* If I become likened to a ray I will be softened, and I am not seeking to be soft. So I will not project any color or hue to anyone until near the end of my time period influence in approximately two years or more. I am not a ray, but I can be its master coordinator, if you comprehend that.

V.   Then ultimately you will relate to the indigo rather than the purple or the blue or the other ray colors?

U.   That is correct. Right now you would not associate me with any definite color. I am concerned about your planet. I am concerned about peace. I am concerned about each lifeform. I can relate to any color if I choose to, but right now I am whitish, gold and silver, and not aligned with any separate color.

V.   Thank you. Now, in terms of our physical earth that we call Terra, or Gaia, could you indicate what your relationship to us has been since the beginning of this planet's creation?

U.   In the beginning while Michael was recruiting etheric energies for this planet and coordinating all details, I was not around at all. There was no apparent concern or reason to be around. Michael had his project. I was over in the western region. Gabriel and Raphael had their work elsewhere. When Michael was assigned this earth project, it was not to be difficult. What actually came about is a totally different story, however. For when we read the files of your small place and try to think of another plan to pull it out of its boiling pot, it is now an immense task.

V.   Did the original etheric souls have relationships with the angelic realm other than Archangel Michael? That is, while they were above and around the planet doing their work, were they able to contact and associate with angels?

U.   Yes. Because your original beings had a high vibrational density they could perceive our dimension. So the answer is that the beings you call angelic and those about the planet's surface did interrelate.

V.   So it would not have been mysterious or unusual in those early days for a slightly, mostly etheric energy soul to be in contact with angelic realms of all kinds?

59

DESCENT OF THE DOVE

U.   That is true. For if you take away your physical body, the soul energy beam remains. Even if you remove the physical density, *you* are there. Therefore, any nearby etheric being could see you very clearly. And it could contact you since you would be beyond the realm of emotions and the limiting density of physicalness. Does that help you?

V.   Thank you. Are there rather distinctive limitations that prevent certain forms from associating with other forms?

U.   Are you speaking of now?

V.   Yes, I am speaking of the universe today. Are we separated from you only because we are in the physical body?

U.   You are level three accelerating to low level four in consciousness. A high 4th level was established in thought and example 2,000 years ago by Jesus the Christ's visit; he showed the possibility of transformation out of 3rd dimensional bondage, even as the Buddha taught before him. When you attain the higher level four and feel its higher vibration, and even see the luminosity of level five, then you begin to turn your perspective totally away from the surface of the planet.

The larger number of earth soul inhabitants will have to go through stages of consciousness education. This education will bring a freedom from the lower 4th dimension's emotional attachment and power connection to the 3rd dimension world called earth living.

Some humans are already freeing themselves by inner cleansing and personality healing and have surpassed the lower 4th dimension thereby achieving high 4th dimension awareness and operating with potential for the 5th. A few have attained lower 5th already. At this period in spiritual evolution, attainment of lower 5th dimension can only be reached by practical actions to heal the planet and bring peace. No one can proceed into higher consciousness at the 5th dimension without participating in Preservation of all Life—Peace on Earth.

V.   So there are some people on the physical planet today who could perceive the 5th dimension?

U.   Yes, especially those who have committed to the planet's well-being and are actually assisting her cleansing. Yet understand that each dimension has a *range* within it.

What I am coming to do now is pierce through the 4th dimension and get right down to the planet's surface. I come to turn you around. I want people to look back up toward the light. I am trying to sweep away the clouds that are over your eyes. We wish to dispel much of the fog so you can see right through to the cosmic energy that is there at the 5th dimension. We want to free you from both 3rd and lower 4th dimensional thinking. I can bring an opening to the 5th dimension for those who cleanse themselves at the personality level and work to bring peace. *I come to end soul-personality duality forever.*

V.   I am almost overwhelmed by this news, this immense gift. Thank you, Uriel. (Long, silent pause.) Is our understanding correct that in the 4th dimension there are still souls that have outlines of physical human bodies?

U.   Yes, in the lower level of the 4th. It would no longer be a human form as you think of it, however. As you get closer to the 5th, it would dissolve again just into energy.

V.   Can you explain how that transpires?

U.   It becomes like an electro-magnetic field; it just occurs by virtue of reaching higher frequency. As you get away from the vibration of the planet you no longer need to relate to its dense vibration. It is rather like taking off one garment for something lighter. It is a propulsion back to a more normal soul state.

V.   When we earth souls had these former seven-foot energy beams, or a soul without a physical body, could we safely travel by ourselves in the universe or at least in this galaxy? Or did we need what is called UFO craft or stellar craft to move?

U.   No, you did not need any craft; you had the ability within yourselves to move to outer space. However, soul beams do not usually traverse great distances very quickly.

V.   In other words, they couldn't do what you and the Great Rays do with ease?

U.   That is correct. A seven-foot energy beam's frequency doesn't have enough power to manipulate itself around the universe.

V.   You say you have come here to help us. Could you describe more about that?

U.   I have been greatly empowered by the Gold Ray and the Silver Ray to use their energies and the rainbow energies already provided by them around the planet's perimeter. This power allows me to utilize the qualities inherent in each ray color and also to have all their combined and magnified power at my disposal.

I will liken each soul to a curved dish or mirror, such as your satellite dishes that receive waves. The waves from the Gold and Silver Rays and myself will come into your soul, be assimilated and then sent back out by the soul into cosmic consciousness. Can you understand this?

V.   Is this light and energy vibration?

U.   Yes. The light and energy of the Gold and the Silver Rays, which although higher than three years ago, is at a relatively low amplification at this time. It will begin to increase, and I will eventually bring further amplification, to a level of 27 to 35%, through myself as a conductor. I do not want to unbalance anyone. However, I am going to make each person feel that something is going on so he or she must notice it and take action. This will affect each person's soul as I focus on a minute portion of the soul energy and make it into a receptive area for potential expansion. Each person will likely feel something.

    V.   Are you saying that the incoming amplified energy of the Great Rays through you will in some way interact with the energy field within our physical bodies?

    U.   Yes. As the physical body is only a soul container, I will relate to the mind and soul knowingness of each person.

    V.   Let me pause here a minute to be sure I grasp this. It is my understanding that each soul was given energy colors in this existence that we call a cosmic soul print or Ray of Intention. Is this to be affected in any way?

    U.   As I work with the amplification of energy, your individual receptivity of acknowledging God with your soul-personality will bring forth one of two effects. Either your Ray of Intention will become activated and energized with more forcefulness, or you will suppress it. Those who truly want to be reverent and want to fulfill their soul's purpose will agree to get all the way into it.

Those who *do not* will still receive the amplification, or zapping as you call it, but it will not do anything because they are choosing to keep it depressed. Their Ray of Intention will still feel it, but whether the soul does anything with it is the big question! I will be endeavoring to make it very difficult for the soul to say "no." By having each one awaken through personal experience all will truly be able to make a decision with wisdom. *A decision made now or during the next two years will not be a "maybe" decision; it must be a "yes" or a "no" for God, for peace.*

V.   Can you indicate, Uriel, how your energy increase will affect those of us who have already said "yes" and are serving?

U.   This will be a time of more work, yet it will be a time of rejoicing because all will truly know what they are doing and why. They will truly feel appreciated and know that we are dedicated to working with them! They will have a sense of being *acknowledged, seen and accepted* and will absolutely know that we are cooperating with them in very real ways.

V.   That brings tears to my eyes. I also wish to ask how those who are already working very hard can physically care for themselves lest in their rush to serve, they become adversely affected.

U.   Yes. There will be many of those who may become involved in intense work, stress and overexertion as you state. You must assist each other to find balance so all will be able to continue on the earth plane and accomplish their goals. Be assured that those few who are soul-programmed to leave earth through the release process will go immediately up through the energy cycles to the levels that have been held open for them. They will then have a very *short review* before starting to work again with this planet. So there is the ability to either continue in the physicalness or (for a few) to leave and go back up to a level of earned attainment.

V.   Uriel, could you say something about the ways the physical body's molecules and the cells will be affected by your energy amplifications?

U.   Let me say this to earth's 5 billion souls. The intake of liquids and food is the primary key here, along with rest and exercise. Your food intake will naturally become smaller and smaller. We will try to get you to utilize the energies of the sea to give you vitality.

The products of the earth's soil are grains, nuts, seeds, fruits and vegetables (also herbs). You will find that as this time progresses, food will become less and less important. I understand you will still need to partake, but it likely will be in different forms. There are those to assist you with development of the sea energy food and energies of the land related to green things. Much information has come, and will soon come, to you about this.

There are two aspects of my present project that I wish to share. (1) *The outpouring of knowledge and information will decrease.* (2) *The outpouring of momentum or energy to move everybody toward peace is going to increase.* So you are going to have a decrease in the outpouring of specific information even though channeled information will seem to be coming from everywhere! Yet with the communication intensity from our realm to yours, actual information will decrease as everybody will be saying, "Hurry up, get together and work to create peace." Some technical information will come as part of the awakening experience that we now focus upon.

From me, and because of me, you are going to see a shift in the pulsation of the energy that motivates and moves people out into activity. Your metaphysical teachers say personal peace within each human must come first, and this is the ideal, yet when your countries geared up for past war efforts, they took workers exactly as they were and went into action from that point. We seek to increase your inner development, of course; however, we must have your action now. The wise will accomplish both.

V.   With an increasing vibration of this magnitude, would it be easier for UFO's and space brothers to give us data?

U.   Space contact existed but did not work in Atlantis, or rather it worked to the detriment of the human beings. Therefore, we are going to use a different approach this time. Since nothing externally applied has worked, we bring the requirement that each soul must now show responsibility for completion of its purpose in a specified time.

V.   Uriel, with such advanced weaponry and war creations, wouldn't your increased energy help some people unlock inner remembrance to even worse weapons, perhaps things they had knowledge of in prior lives?

U.   The effect of my energy will have such an outgoing, zig-zag push or impact that it could unlock some destructiveness. Yet human destructiveness is *not* going to work. It will not accomplish the goals that individuals wish, and they are going to see that all it brought about was harm. That is an aspect of the required change of consciousness.

We cannot take away your free will factor because it is built into the human body design and is supported by the planetary environment. It is an agreement as part of the Silver Ray's pattern. So, some destructiveness could happen, yet it will not be global. Out of these pockets of destructiveness will come the human perception that destructiveness has no value.

However, sound frequency and hydrogen misuse must be controlled, which is why you have our full attention and support. We are here to guide, explain and assist in applying the soul's purpose toward correct physical solutions. The involvement of the soul itself will begin to have its affect by demanding preservation of its personal body and all other life as well. Thus you will find that although there may be some actual destructiveness, or the potential of destructiveness, much of that will *not* occur.

There will be a definite wave of change that will happen in the next 14 months, for we have started the energy at a very low wattage. I am endeavoring to have the message regarding my purpose be known as soon as possible. Even as we say 14 months, you must understand we do not have time measurement and can only forecast *probabilities*. None of us will say that at 10:00 o'clock, May 15th, you will have peace—or catastrophe.

But you may be certain that your perception of time will eventually cease to exist, since it is an error. Yes, you will soon be aware that the equation of past-present-future is inaccurate. Dear friends, the plan has begun. Your limited linear time is vanishing . . . and with it, the rigid structures of your 3rd dimension reality. You now approach the only true reality, which is the state of cosmic consciousness or awareness—the home of God's love and your only joyful expression.

As stated, many things are happening simultaneously. You will be increasingly aware of the *importance of existence* in your life. Each day's activities, each day's experiences, will have more (or less) emphasis as you evaluate what is or is not necessary. *Prioritize unceasingly.* Let go of everything but peaceful intention. The value of your life and its quality will be increased! You will finally perceive the value of yourself as a Christed being of light living out galactic law and the Creator's will in a physical life existence, until you join us once again in harmonious consciousness.

Rejoice, cousins of mine! Your spiritual evolution sings new coordinates of life in the only non-illusionary homeland possible.

Peace to every heart and soul.

Chapter IV

Positive and Negative Thought

Many people believe that by their positive thoughts they can "overcome" the evil or negative thoughts of others. Some even assume that, if ignored, negativity does not exist and cannot affect them at all.

Let us begin this discussion by stating that your thoughts *do* create a force field around you. This force field can be highly charged with a positive quality, up to a distance of 20 feet outward. A pure energy field feels vibrant and healing to others but does not necessarily influence their attitudes or action. If you are filled with and can maintain this high energy, you will feel superb! Regrettably, most humans maintain a very low force field of only 12 to 18 inches with occasional bursts up to two to four feet. Concentrated brain wave patterns of 7.8 megahertz per second are achievable through meditation and can expand a normally low force field, if consistently done, by up to one-half to one inch per day until the 20-foot range is reached. Because of lack of use of the brain's thinking process, at large, there will be some people who will take longer to achieve and maintain 7.8 to 8.0 megahertz per second brain wave patterns during meditation.

Continual daily meditation in the 7.8 to 8.0 megahertz range maintains this status, once it has been achieved, in spite of the strong negative energies most of you exist in. Because we observe that humans with low noise pollution have a purer quality and stronger amplification, we urge you to avoid loud noise and distinctive audible and inaudible sound frequencies. Especially avoid consistent and repetitive ones that can lower physical health and affect mental and emotional well being. The smaller your energy field the more likely you will experience emotional upset, mental confusion or even become subject to negative thought input. A stronger electrical field is a form of spiritual armor, so to speak.

Beyond that original 20-foot radius the force field intermingles with other objects due to a decrease in its vitality. A high-quality personal force field must be achieved and maintained in these busy days with the excessive noise pollution most city dwellers are bombarded with. Your greatest spiritual teachers have had personal force fields up to four miles in radius, becoming less vibrant at their perimeter but still observable and harmonious in their quality. This gives you an idea of the human spiritual potential that once again may be attainable.

A "negative" thought energy can also be powerful in its amplification, extending a similar distance, because that person feels good and sure about him or herself. Then you may wonder where the difference is. The process is the same except for the intention and the subsequent *physical* actions taken.

When a thought has emotions or feelings with it, a reality is registered within the brain and it becomes an experience just as if you had actually done a deed. Otherwise it is merely a functional analysis and calculation of information.

A physical action involves many of your senses and becomes very real to the brain, your thought center, even without strong emotional content. You feel and experience the

70

action even if you were not aware of or not alert to it. Everything is being registered or recorded as real. This is why under hypnosis you can describe all the details even though you cannot consciously recall them. You have experienced the total event as far as the brain is concerned. There are so many aspects of the human body design you are just now realizing. You truly do create your own inner world even as you live in outer group consciousness, *provided there is no E.L.F. interference at the physical world level.*

For those humans not familiar with the term E.L.F., let me explain that when you hear sound it has a frequency range—sometimes high and sometimes low. Sounds that have an Extremely Low Frequency are capable of healing the human body, as the 7.8 to 8.0 range achieved in meditation demonstrates. However, these low energy frequency currents can also be misused to cause brain wave confusion, physical, mental and emotional debilitation and *deadly* genetic distortion.

My role in this document is not to be your scientific advisor, but these E.L.F. horror weapons are being used by at least two major governments. The Soviet Union was the first; then the United States sought a defense against these mortally dangerous weapons. Be informed about these horrendous weapons and take action to stop them! Insane minds are clearly at work.

That which you call evil has its own reality, power and intention just as positive does. If you are praying for peace or cessation of nuclear testing but planetary destructiveness continues because many are warlike in thought and deed, you are ignoring the reality of your physical plane existence. Within matter each action is a reality. The reality has substance and is *real* because it exists, whether it be as a thought or a manifested, actual matter form. It exists because of the energy given to it.

Therefore, friend, it is important that you become involved in action for Preservation of all Life—Peace on Earth *now*. The hydrogen and nuclear testings, the E.L.F. devices and horrendous machines of warfare must be physically eliminated. That action is critical. The many forms of pollution that exist must also be attended to on your physical plane of existence by physical actions.

These harmful situations will not go away by themselves or by thought alone, because they are constantly being fed and energized by repetitive use. Events or situations that go away do so either by not being repeated or by adapting to environments when the continued forward energy thrust is removed.

You are to be fully aware that *cause and effect* is a very powerful tool. It exists for *all* things! The effects of your tomorrows are in your causes of today. Your past errors are here to haunt you even now. As time does not exist the effects today can be from causes months or years ago. This cause and effect can be on an individual basis or a planetary one.

That which is called negative is powerful and dense. It seems to be heavier than the positive vibrations. The negative energy can be around a person, place or thing. It can hang in an area where you can both feel and see it. You are not imagining when you think you feel, sense or see energies; they *are* there!

After your fall from high soul energy to very low energy, a physical body was created to keep your soul safe. Your original physical form was totally pure and had no negative aspects. These were acquired by later experience within an environment where negativity has been added to influence you. This original negativity came from a former holy light being who subsequently chose not to revere its Creator. It is

72

real. I am real. You are real. Negative energies are real! Not to be feared, for that is self-defeating. Yet they must be understood and taken into consideration.

This Time of Awakening comes to awaken your knowledge about thought as energy, which will allow you to move forward in action to recreate the happiness intended within the divine construct of peace and harmony on your planet.

Although you consider many third plane "things" — such as trees, flowers, plants, even a human—illusions, this is not fully correct. Order of movement is a universal law. Each thing has its own cycle of existence, its pattern of behavior. This pattern is within a cycle that gives the thing energy and existence, substance, and a form of reality. This reality exists for a tree, a human or a sequence of atomic movement. Each thing is an existence of energy in some form; therefore, it is real!

As you grasp this you will more clearly understand the immediate need for action both as an individual and as a member of an immense planetary family. Within your plane of existence *all things* relate to each other. The circles are there within each other. The spiral of illumination is going upward, but it is also coming downward to you as information for consideration and edification.

We are aware of the metaphysical belief on your planet that if you truly think only positive, highly focused thoughts, you can totally control the events of your life. Many are learning that by becoming expert in this mind control process nothing adverse can affect them. Thus you become the "master of your fate," so to speak, while incarnated in a physical body.

Sometimes this state is referred to as being a co-creator with God or using the Higher Self or soul power. Such a belief is partially accurate, and we applaud those teachers who have introduced the concept so that each soul and its humanness might truly be allowed an avenue through which its yearnings and purpose can express in material form.

However, in our observation of how this "new thought" process works for you, may I state these comments for your consideration? Frankly, by our present calculation, only an extremely proficient, long-standing user of these methods can attain anything like 75 to 80% control of his or her personal thoughts and affairs, although several living teachers and those you call practitioners have reached a high of 92%.

"New thought" is still a very fine concept, nonetheless, and a needed accomplishment that all earth dwellers could emulate. Certainly we of the angelic realms will join with your spiritual masters and teachers to support such a movement in positive thinking for all of humanity during the Time of Awakening. To do this, we have decided to discuss several aspects of this thought process topic as it relates to your particular 3rd dimensional planet.

The unity of God's creative intention is not merely conceptual or mental. It contains within its purpose and capability the architecture for the physical manifestation of the event, object, or lifeform to occur. In fact, unless the physical aspect is completed and brought into reality, "the word," as some have called it, is not allowed its unity, or oneness, to be manifested. In your dimension, then, your planet is real. You are real. The trees and animals and minerals are all physical outcomes of original God-intention.

In your level of life, all of this is true, yet this is an "illusion" in that you do not see each thing as composed of *energy.* Thus, a table is not a solid or dense object, but is composed of energy of molecular atoms. You have presently limited perception, then, regarding the unified energy process that has caused its manifestation. Thus, your ignorance regarding the power and intention of God's vision prevents your understanding of the total process of creation. You are seeing only one part of that creative vision, which might be called the "finished product." Your planetary or physical residence is not an illusion, though you are blind to its probable longevity and its true purpose, because you have cemented it with a linear belief structure you call time.

Simply put, the physical reality of the universe, galaxy, solar system and planet has both a mind pattern and a physical manifestation expression; therefore, you are affected in the physical world by the power, actions and reactions of other physical things. Regardless of where you focus your mind awareness or consciousness there will be some effects on your physical condition caused by the thinking and actions of others since the *free will* aspect of human lifeforms is still permitted on your planet.

What does this mean to you personally? It means that until the planet is totally cleansed of the accumulated and com-pacted negative thinking, you will have to take *physical actions* for peace. You cannot create change merely by believing in its concept and/or by meditating and praying for peace. BOTH thought and action are necessary and that is why we have come. It is my task to assist humanity's movement into *physical acts of service*, and thereby help resolve the many physical problems your planet presently has.

I said earlier that while some metaphysicians can control the majority of their own individual life experiences by positive thinking and action, there is still no massive plane-tary movement for positive thought or action. Rather, and I relate this with empathy of soul feeling, *only 12 to 18% of your population actually work for peace*, though over half would say they believe in peace. The majority of those who speak about their concerns are not putting their words into practice. This inconsistency is what must change!

That is why you, as individuals, are not able to fully control your lives. There are some truly evil beings who hold powerful positions of control and authority. To deny this is folly! There are also many on the planet who are totally unfocused on peace. This group is a great majority who complacently await God, Jesus, angels, or a super being to save them from their personal responsibility of corrective, physical action. Be assured we are here to help change all this, and to fully honor and acknowledge those of you who are already empowering your concerns with physical action and deeds. Yet it is you who must act physically and persuade others to do the same. Helpless feelings diminish when you move into useful activities.

Need I point out that each human, animal, bird, plant or mineral is part of one family, and you humans are the obligatory, primary caretakers of it all? You were long ago given that sacred responsibility, and we now ask each of you to remember and focus fully on that necessary dominion.

Your thoughts alone, without energy output toward practical solutions, are presently incapable of turning the tide. Even your 12% combined pure thoughts for peace cannot stop any massive physical event such as an exploding missile or underground hydrogen explosion. You cannot prevent intense earth movements created by E.L.F. waves, levitate physical objects, or even keep a tall uprooted tree from falling. Yet you can do much both as an individual and as a group member within a variety of organizations and alliances that are achieving purposeful action for peace.

Through this higher awareness you can change the consciousness behind human decisions that create planetary deterioration and possible disintegration. Since the planet, you and all things on it have physical form, you must become a

worker for the very core of God's intention for life continuance. This is your goal and ours. Peace is not an illusion;
however, the casual belief that it takes no personal action to
cure your ills is definitely illusory.

Beyond the insanity of destructive E.L.F. waves, underground hydrogen explosions and the many nuclear and atomic
weapons, you have despoiled the planet itself. Humanity has
damaged the oxygenation process for clean breathing, poi-
soned the thirst-quenching water and tampered with God's
elements in space. I remind you that none of this will go away
by thought alone. Release ignorance and arrogance! Begin the
needed physical changes, rehabilitations, and restitutions by
your own efforts. We can and will support your clarity of
purpose, give you our wisdom, guidance and energy, but the
labor and commitment are yours alone to supply. You are
earth dwellers and custodians. We will help you, but the
responsibility of physical actions is under human aegis.

Given your many choices how can you best meet this
challenge?

The key is group effort and responsibility. Within the
positive thought attitude is the ingredient of working with
energy so that you integrate yourself with the outer, cosmic
energy. You must impress your own self-contained energies
positively, of course, and then connect your positive energies
with others who likewise wish to cooperate for peace.

If you ask, "Does an individual in group meditation have
the power to influence other people, other circumstances, and
the potentiality of events simply by mental activity or spiritual
thought intervention?" the answer is, "Yes, but not totally."
Yet the thought process that you use to put information out
into God's cosmic energy, which is around everything, will
blend and participate. Once the thought is there, its
unmanifested potential is available.

77

The recommended process at this time would be to have immense numbers of humans simultaneously agree on peace (as you do only once or twice a year now) and then *sustain their thoughts through action*. Of course, to cause the neutralizing of your destructive devices you would need at least 32 to 37% of your entire population to simultaneously focus their positive peace attitudes. This alone could change the electrical field of the planet unless your scientists are willing to use their E.L.F. technology to neutralize or abort destructive devices.

As I mentioned, only 12 to 18% of your 5-plus billion people are participating in actual peace work. We need more! The issue that we will repeatedly emphasize is that each person must translate empty words into action-oriented intentions or accomplishments.

Since your consistency fluctuates between that 12 and 18% intention, urgent change is required immediately. It cannot wait. If I seem redundant it is because I care. The stockpile of your destructive devices is immense. Even when something in your weapon technology becomes obsolete, that does not disarm the device. What must occur is that the masses become totally involved with halting new weapons, neutralizing present weapons and ceasing any possibility of future destructiveness through thought or deed.

The age of global communication presently available means you can educate large territories or areas of population very quickly. You can teach the positive thought process to children and adults. You can visually demonstrate to large numbers the potential nuclear destructiveness, as a few TV, radio and movie presentations have done already. You can be ready with follow-up contacts.

If a protest is planned, have a documentary beforehand with media publicity stating the views and explanation about why the protest is being made. A few words or statements as shown on placards or banners do not give the thorough level of explanation needed. Some are working diligently along these lines, but more work is required.

You have over 5,000 organizations that are already formed for peace. Call these organizations together for a *common plan of action!* We need the exponential power of their mutual efforts. Join together you must. This cooperation is vital, truly vital. By these commitments you can change the planet's tragedy to joy very quickly, as we lend our immense support. Our vibrations incite change within everyone who wants to be energized into constructive action. We add to your purity of heart intention for non-destructiveness.

There was a time when you did not have the destructive devices as they are now known. By not voicing opposition and *taking* preventative actions, that destructiveness was allowed to grow, develop and sink its roots into your belief systems. Now that belief system of attack and defend, defend and attack, has taken control of most human behavior.

Major nations fear one another, and as those opponents spend fortunes on military materials and personnel, the smaller nations watch nervously. No peace is possible in this arena of distrust. Living with a banked fire about to blaze out of control, you wait and worry. This situation is not the plan expected by your spiritual realms.

So many great teachings have said that distrust and fear are ungodly! All have spoken of love or compassion and harmlessness as keys to peace. What nation has courage and conviction to practice humanitarian belief? greater trust? What humans will model the principles your churchmen preach?

The truth of metaphysics now challenges outmoded religious practices, for there is no true religion other than the spiritual awareness of God and application of God qualities. God is peacefulness, harmony and cooperation. *To say that peacefulness is important to you and not live it is contradictory and counterproductive.*

Your fear of war with each other causes loss of peace, but you never resolve the cause. Fear about possible earthquakes leads you to seek information about survival. You ask and ask and ask us how you should prepare for possible earth changes. You wonder if you will be safe. Why will you not seek to do something about the cause of destructiveness and war which is, after all, the most logical solution? For if you remove fear and hate—the primary causes of war—through respect and caring, you neutralize or balance the anger level on earth. Then why not put effort where it counts the most and survive through love, caring and cooperation as a planetary family?

You are not helpless unless you choose to be. You have many models to follow such as Krishna, the Buddha, Old Testament prophets, Lord Jesus and more recent spiritual teachers by many names. You have as many ancient ones who are not historically recorded as you do those you claim to remember and honor. Unity is your true salvation, therefore, because gathering together as a collective unit of power with focused agreement creates exponential results.

You might ask if some individuals have more power to amplify their own energy intention than others, and the answer is "yes." However, they do not make up for the ones who are not as powerful. Again, I suggest you realize that each individual is an electrical unit. Even if you speak for someone else, the electrical energy of that person is still not involved. You cannot constantly be responsible for another person's electrical energy field usage. Even if free will were not a factor, you cannot amplify the force field of your own energy to last for the months or years that would be necessary.

This time is a period when each individual must be responsible for him or herself. Indeed, each soul must account for itself *now*, as well it knows.

You, as a global or spheric community in space, must grasp the concept that, although you are a soul still containing some of God's creative energy and ability, *you cannot recreate the physical earth if you destroy it physically.* Due to the extended periods of negativity, the thought climate around your planet is currently very putrid. It would take somewhere around 200,000 years (in your time measurement) if all of you had a combined peace thought but took no action to implement it in everyday life. In other words, positive thought is not enough, and it would take far too long to accomplish total reversal of the compacted negativity around the planet.

In addition, since your technological discoveries are horrendously outpacing spiritual integrity, and your present population explosion will advance to 6 billion people within two decades, those two reasons alone would increase the 200,000-year task to about a 327,000-year task of renovation. Again, I must say that you do not have enough time for the thought process alone. The situation has become too critical. This also assumes you would avoid further wars using atomic and nuclear devices, your "new horror" weapons, and also further hydrogen explosions.

When you experience this information without fear and perceive that we have come to guide and assist you through your energy invention's misuse, you can rejoice. Since you have too many weapons and a continuing desire for war, we must make some rapid changes, however. When a pot is boiling over, you move fast. With our high spiritual consciousness to help change your beliefs, you will rise in purposeful commitment and physical service consistently focused with inspiration for practical accomplishment.

It is true you cannot accomplish this alone, for your planet is endangered and represents an immense danger to yourselves and others. You have prayed for help, have you not? And we have come with a divine plan to regain the nobility of life as it was known here so long ago.

Now, let me pause for any questions you wish to ask.

V.   Some people say they can't seem to know God or that they feel separated from God. Is the experience of separation from God real or an illusion?

U.   God essence is always there . . . always. When you feel any separation, it is your own soul feeling a lack of its fine tuning to consciousness and Universal Mind, and thus to all other life that exists. The feeling of separateness from the God essence is not an illusion to the one choosing disconnection and needs not be a permanent condition. When this illusion is very potent you speak of "the dark night of the soul." Humans who do not change this perception are terribly troubled. It is because the thought process (the individual's brain-intelligence synchronization with the soul) is so distorted that the soul is not perceiving the other dimensions where God is the manifested reality.

V.   So within its own reality it is having an illusion that doesn't exist?

U.   We would not perceive it as an illusion. We would perceive it as frequency interference or perception interference.

V.   In other words all beings on this planet could be having the experience of oneness with God, and that is not an illusion?

U.   Yes. As with all perception, you have made a choice, and sometimes you choose to exist with blinders on. God and cosmic energy are constant. You are not

82

separate from it because you always are in it. It is your perception that is distorted.

V.   Could you comment on the metaphysical belief that we co-create all of our experiences and that everything that happens to us actually has some relationship to our own thought pattern? Some say that because of the law of attraction every experience has our consent, and we will never have an experience in which we have not agreed to participate, even if it is totally subconscious.

U.   The law of attraction can be overridden by free will because you are a community of 5 billion humans living together. Each individual is constantly interacting with one or many other individuals on the planet. Therefore, when anyone is physically moving, that person is usually in someone else's electrical field. When an automobile strikes your vehicle, several elements are involved. One, a car is a solid mass. It is moving forward. (The example is forward, not backward, yet even going backwards is a forward motion.) The automobile is also moving within the electrical field of one or more other vehicles or individuals. If a person is struck (even hurt) by that out-of-control vehicle, understand that they did not attract it like a physical magnet. That vehicle is driven by someone with free will. If the driver is drunk and crashes into you, your vehicle is within a sequence of physical events. You merely happen to be there, so you are within the cause and effect of another person's moving vehicle. You have not attracted yourself to its electrical field like a magnet. Although it is called electro-magnetic field, that does not mean you are attached to it like a magnet that holds you to the planet so that you will not fall off or float away.

V.   Then we are still capable of true accidents? And may experience things that we can't always control?

U.   Sometimes. The more you interact with many people in many places the more you could have an inadvertent experience. The law of attraction has validity, yet it is not 100% applicable on earth because of the excessive negativity here. The purer the total environment, the greater the law can manifest. There are many areas of pleasure and difficulty that you experience here as a human, due to the low vibration on your planet.

Metaphysics is most helpful in clarifying that the use of brain thought works in conjunction with its own intellectual desires. Thought impulses from the brain synchronize the human body's physical activities to fulfill desires that have been generated by the intellect. Even when you think you are not doing anything, you have sent a message within the intelligence that you wish a desired result to occur. On both levels you begin to control the desired results in and beyond the body. Your body is a machine, and the machine is responding to the directive that it has received. But everyone else is also thinking ideas simultaneously. Therefore, confusion and difficulty are possible. The more all of you use peaceful thinking and practice positive actions, the higher the percent of your personal control and planetary unity.

V.   Would you say more about that?

U.   Yes. This law of attraction is a utilization of the intellect's directive to fulfill its desires. It accomplishes this by sending out messages through the senses and electrical field of the body. Emotions intensify the message and its potential effects. There is a constant communication of information between personality desire and the brain's function to complete or fulfill the intention. When your

total body function focuses on finding a solution or fulfillment it turns with its senses and begins to search for the
source of fulfillment.

V.   Are you speaking now about the subconscious
influences or conscious mind influence?

U.   It becomes both. Because of the complexities of
electrical current and the human as a multi-level machine,
it must be understood that some thoughts are in a development stage while others are on their way to completion. In
other words, thoughts go out in a continuing series. The
internal or subconscious process is developmental and
involves research through memory banks to fulfill its
request. The closer the desire comes into expression, the
more conscious the level of awareness within the individual. An example of this would be that while you are eating,
driving or walking—some physical activity—you are also
thinking about a vacation you'd like, or the new coat you
need—something you desire. The brain proceeds to bring
your desire into fruition by seeking out the way this could
occur—where to go, what to do, and so on. This is the
multi-dimensional aspect of the human activity. You are
doing one thing but thinking about several other things
almost simultaneously. The brain seldom rests; its activity
goes on constantly. You could have over 1,000 activities
going on every instant, in or out of your conscious
awareness, just to carry out bodily functions and life's
activities. As Silver Ray states, you are an incredibly
complicated machine. Soon you will learn what you really
are as a created form, and what to do with all you are.

V.   You said multi-dimensional. How many dimensions are you counting here?

U.   You can have an awareness of seven at one time
rather than just the five physical senses you have identified.

Each of the five is physical with perception capabilities to higher dimensions, as well. Even when you are aware of using your physical senses, or of being in the physical dimension, you are also working with the spiritual level of some or all of the senses. Two or more become multi-dimensional.

V.   Most of us know about the five physical senses, but you say we have seven.

U.   On scientific levels you may hear of nine or more physical dimensions, but these are not *spiritual*.

V.   What are the other two by your definition?

U.   Spiritual awareness or spiritual discernment is one and second, conceptual alignment of intellect with the soul itself, is what you call enlightenment. Physical sight, taste, touch, smell and hearing are mainly focused on everyday material world events. Whereas the other two are of what you would term things of the spirit.

V.   Could you further clarify the higher two?

U.   Yes. There is the soul's spiritual discernment, which is relating to information in the other dimensions beyond the physical body, such as invisible light beings outside of the body. The second is seeking to bring the brain-intellect function under the soul's control for completion of earth tasks.

V.   So if we went up in order of senses, then the one beyond the five physical senses, which I presume we call the 6th sense, is when the soul is able to bring each physical sense to a purer intention in harmony with its own purpose.

U.   Yes.

V.   Then the one beyond that, called the 7th sense, is the ability to go beyond the physical senses and their higher

86

spiritual knowing, to connect the soul with Universal Mind and its greater consciousness?

U.   Yes.

V.   Returning to your earlier comment that our own personal thoughts do not always prevail in life because of the present earth negativity and free will factor—the idea seems to make us quite vulnerable. To be at the effect of anything and everything that could happen is a very scary proposition.

U.   Agreed. And you generally perceive only a few solutions out of that fear. One solution is to expect God to save you since only God has any true or ultimate power. Many people hope that if their actions are reverent, they will be protected by God and various helpers such as Lord Jesus, angels, and so forth. Many humans conclude that you should stay on the "good side" of the powerful ones, because only they can keep you safe.

This fear of unknown events is so very deeply imbedded in humanity that when you are in a physical body many of you experience great misery. A mountain avalanche could come down, or a person could accidentally, or even deliberately, hurt or kill you. So much of your life is lived in fear and defensiveness against the unknown—things you have no control over. So you believe in God to help you; you ask Jesus or your angels to make life safe.

Another solution to your fear is to take the attitude that nothing matters anyway so why not do whatever you wish? Be ruthless, loveless. Take control. Then you are safely in charge.

A more recent theory, mentioned earlier, is the perception that with positive mental attitude you are not really at the effect of anything. You accept that you really are very powerful and what you think attracts like, thus acquiring

security in your physical body and life events by controlling the environment. This way you can avoid what you call
fate or negative destiny. However, you then are made to feel
guilty, or a failure, if anything untoward or painful occurs,
is this correct? For you have done something ''wrong'' and
let this painful thing happen.

V.   Very!

U.   My comments are that the concept of positive
thinking is excellent. Within your own reality you do have
many more positive effects returning. If you spend years in
successful study for a college degree, it is earned. If you
consistently take drugs and alcohol there will be physical
effects. These are obvious causes and you perceive the
connection, accept the responsibility. Your dilemma comes
when you cannot make sense of an event and must assign
blame or responsibility somewhere. Then you can blame
either fate, God, yourself, the devil or the other parties
involved, as you choose. Very few can say and mean, ''It
just happened,'' and proceed with any sense of true peace.

Your fear factor is not only within yourself but also
around the planet. Thus do you plan for safety by defendand-attack measures. You may even blame the devil for the
difficulties experienced as an individual, as a group or as a
humanity. But even the Rebel Ray cannot be blamed for
everything! Can you view humanity's cosmic debt as a
planetary citizen and see that planetary problems are
mostly caused by humanity?

V.   That's interesting. Now, what is the average person who wants to work for peace to do? How much control
do we have over our own life events in this time period?

U.   The factor of free will continually exists. That is
one of the alignments that the soul is constantly working
on. Free will means choosing whether or not to revere God

and the divine plan for life on this planet. Free choice is how you personally carry out your part in that. It means selecting the particular way you will do that. One might be a teacher, another a nurse. One might marry, another remain single, and so forth. Free will is the matrix, and your choices support your primary focus on reverence for God. Interrelating with a multitude of other human life energies causes difficulties in achieving 100% control of your own life events even when you've made a free will decision to revere God. The soul itself continues to implement its free will choice, yet by virtue of quantity you are interacting with other energies so often that you have to constantly adjust your free choice. This causes the soul difficulties because it knows what it wants to do; however, the intellect is working with an abundance of information coming into it at once, including interference from others. It therefore experiences confusion as to the most viable choices it might make.

The overriding of anyone's free will and free choice causes difficulty (karma) for the one who does the overriding. One of the points that has to be brought out during this Time of Awakening is that each person makes many adjustments in everyday living due to the enormously high earth population. This causes stress depending on the inner harmony of the whole being.

V.   Then how much control do we really have in our everyday life? And does the quality of our intention and ability to stay more focused than others give us an advantage?

U.   Those who are not involved in much external physical activity at the moment, or who are in a high degree of control over their environment and life's

89

sequence of events, are less affected by free will intervention from others. Therefore, they are in greater control of the life events in relationship to the possible negative occurrences. Again I would estimate that a very mentally positive person could have 80% control of personal existence in non-war times. Almost all lose personal free will when government allows high violence to rule the land, however. War is an abomination.

When you are not with a large group of active people, you have a higher level of personal control. This control is also supported when you are only among people who are favorable to peace and do not try to take away your free will or oppose you. I remind you once again that you are electrical energy. If you have electrical batteries or electrical machines that are giving off current, and these machines are working in an orderly, harmonious manner, they are synchronized. When the electrical charges become static, you have difficulties.

V.   There seems to be a dichotomy between surrendering the human ego to God's will versus taking on thought control measures for oneself . . . even positive ones. Could you comment?

U.   Yes, and then we must close. Elsewhere in this document is the clarification that the personality (ego) is actually the intelligence field of the body. Therefore, the word "ego" is inappropriate. If you mean you are bringing into alignment your full Self (internal and external expression) with the reverence-for-God factor uppermost, that would be accurate. I realize some of your books use personality and ego as word descriptions or labels of who you are as a non-soul, but there is actually no such separated thing as a person or an ego. When you use those words, you are identifying an accumulated program of electro-magnetic input or information that has been localized in an intelligence field. In the near future you will be learning more of these things. Perhaps you could begin thinking of yourself as a soul with a vehicle that has a certain composition and requirements for maintenance? And capabilities that have not been brought under free soul control? The body and its connective brain and mind functions are for soul use only ... not the other way around.

In my time with you I will strive to have you understand your soul capabilities and the alignment that is necessary between soul activity, bodily functions and intelligence.

I, Uriel, bring an immense soul compassion to your current environmental predicament and mortal challenge. My presence is an act of angelic faith that you *will succeed* and one sun-bright day inhabit many star systems beyond this sparkling earth gem of inordinate beauty and potential.

Some souls may wish to remain here in the coming Time of Radiance. However, we will need many in your form who can practice caring and harmony in novel group situations elsewhere in this universe. For, as you were told, your God has many realms, levels and dimensions of life far beyond your rainbow, far into the starlight, and far across the spectrum of cosmic realities still only pregnant in your dreams.

Those unconscious dreams are sparkling and dancing with wordless truths and gargantuan opportunities, my cousins in flesh. Please advance toward the potential ecstasies inherent in the nature of that One who deemed we should have energy, life and purposefulness to live and write the stardust memoirs intended by creation.

Salutations and caring of the Creator be with you, then, both in this dimension and beyond time. We are answering your soul desire for help in changing a planet's destiny.

Do you remember asking for assistance? Will you immediately set about your vital task of custodianship and dominion?

Chapter V

Worship

The primary intention of this chapter is to emphasize that any present form of worship on the planet is not to be used as an excuse for lack of participation in the practical activities of peace. Any belief in an all-powerful being such as God, a savior, or any form such as an angel does *not* relieve you of responsibility for your own soul accountability and personal conduct. We affirm you are a responsible God-created energy living on a planet that needs *your* care and support and that you are capable of completing your soul's purpose here for peace.

The second intention of this chapter is to open up your mental capabilities to perceive intra-dimensional functions of life on this planet both in its environment, and in relationship to the higher cosmic dimensions from which it came. As a soul embodied in flesh you have obligations and opportunities at both levels.

We have noticed that throughout the eons of human civilization you have developed modes of conduct, religious and spiritual guidelines, moral laws and rituals that remove humanity from the full responsibility of personal actions. You have developed a belief system that usually excuses you as the cause of later experiences and from responsibility for the results that occur to you and all life on the planet.

When events are extremes of either joyfulness or pain you assign the cause to God. If there are famines, God brought them in punishment. If harvests are bountiful, God is beneficent. Are you well acquainted with this thinking? In fact, God has had very little to do with any of these events, and we of the invisible realms must deal with the pervasive ignorance around your planet in this Time of Awakening.

You often use so-called religious beliefs as a justification for taking away the free will of others, sometimes to the point of murder and/or war. As one who has a true reverence for God, however, and one who wishes to demonstrate it in your daily activities, you will seek to live in *harmony* with other human forms, plants, the animal family and the planet itself.

True worship is the manifested demonstration of reverence for The Source in everyday activities. This worship can be either as an individual or a collective experience by two or more persons. The ultimate goal of worship is to see beyond any physical ritual or stylized religious form and be in the greater awareness of Universal Mind completeness. Worship is reaching a state of inter-dimensional awareness, and then using that awareness through the thought process to manifest positive action. It is an act of harmony.

Like a warm caressing breeze this positive action can protect the flowered faces of a garden, heal a small child's injury, yet stand in love before a majority group's belief in violence and depose its power once and for all.

Angelic worship is difficult for me to describe to you, for I am a light of God's creation without a physical body. I have never been out of that light, never been tempted by the darkness. How then, my cousin, can I assist you who have suffered so greatly in negativity and pain on your return to remembrance of your true estate?

94

I can explain that true worship allows you to reach beyond what is evident before your eyes and ''see'' with the mind's intelligence and the soul's inter-dimensional awareness into realities previously hidden. And I can reiterate that you are now moving into an inner level of the Time of Awakening, which has two primary aspects—linear and spiral. If you can perceive your relationship to the planet and all life here in a constructive way, you surely will have attained *intra-dimensional* awareness, which is that *linear* aspect and *spiral*, which is the *inter-dimensional* aspect.

Linear means that you see with your eyes and use your senses in conjunction with what is seen, viewing what seems to be an actual thing or object. Linear thinking has you taking each event in steps. Spiral means you see the thing with the eyes and with your understanding or comprehension, then you are able to discern other possibilities of the object and its place in the system of life. With spiral perception you open up to the wholeness of anything.

Because true worship is a blending of intra-dimensional and inter-dimensional, so that they become one, I will clarify these points in some detail. But it is the reverence for the Creator that holds it all together. Please attend my words carefully, for it is in your application of these two perceptions that we can allow humanity a rapid movement to a higher 4th dimensional consciousness—a great and novel opportunity!

Some humans may see the planet's problems and assist only at that intra-dimensional level without truly relating it in any way to God. These lack the requirement of *reverence*. Others who call themselves spiritual may say they revere heaven's realm, yet they do absolutely nothing to heal and nurture a desperate planetary situation. These lack the requirement of *action. True worship is both reverence and action!*

95

Since you are on the 3rd dimension, you are being asked to interrelate with nature and all life contained within the planet's existence. You can acquire an attitude of parental or soulful caretaking for all aspects of life here on earth by fully understanding each thing that exists and sustains you. Truly you can become eager to nurture it all and preserve it from deterioration and harm.

Through intra-dimensional understanding you may use soul perception to look at a tree and to see its solid mass, then further within the solid mass to its cells and molecules and all substance that makes up the tree. There are limbs, leaves and roots in its design. The soul can also see through the bark into its core to honor the tree's individual function, at the same time acknowledging it as an object on the planet that serves a greater purpose of oxygenating other living things.

Intra-dimensional awareness, then, is perceiving all earth life, so that you are aware of each living thing in this beautiful and divine creation.

Please contemplate this information and allow your soul to surge forth in love and affection for this earth you call home. Your soul understands the *wholeness* of planetary existence here, which is the intra-relationship of everything in unity. In that oneness is vitality and cohesiveness. The blossom of the flower cannot exist without the stem. The stem needs the roots; the roots need the soil or water, whichever is giving it nutrients for the continuance of life.

This growth process needs either the sun's warmth, or for those night blooming creations, energy that bounces off the moon with its nighttime light. Truly begin to experience planet earth and all that exists here. Earth is not my home, yet its beauty deeply communicates to me. Let it communicate to you, and nurture it! Then you can appreciate the higher realms of non-physical reality called inter-dimensional. Here are the celestial multicolored waves of light and energy going through the cosmos, sparkling with God essence and dancing melodious notes of solo and choral performance. Appreciating your earth home fully allows you to look up and out beyond the surface of the planet to the molecular marvels in cosmic energy.

My realms are the spirals or inter-dimensional ones. This is my place of worship (reverence) and consciousness of the light. And you are approaching a reawakening to your own spiritual experiences in that light. That wondrous opportunity should bring immense solace and joy.

So behold the beauty of your created soul as it relates to the unspeakable beauty of cosmic energy. Here in the God-reality that sustains us all with energy so we will have peace and harmony, there is also what you term the quality of love.

Can you stop the mental activity and step into the richness of love for just a moment?

★ ★ ★ ★ ★ ★ ★ ★ ★ ★ ★ ★

How does love feel?

★ ★ ★ ★ ★ ★ ★ ★ ★ ★ ★ ★

These inter-dimensional excursions are critical to bringing a synchronization of soul and intelligence together. In this marriage of soul and physicalness is true human expression.

You have multitudes of people who are engaged in various forms of worship. Many acknowledge a higher being, and some actually use the term God. THEY SAY THEIR WORDS: THEY SAY THEY ARE RELIGIOUS. YET WHAT IS THE BEHAVIOR WE SEE? Certainly not action for peace and salvation of a planet!

It is important that what you say and what you do be in harmony. They must balance. If you say that you revere God yet do not take care of this planet, your words are hollow, for the soul is not involved. The soul is an energy that wishes to be active. In fact, energy cannot maintain itself doing nothing. Energy is vitality, and vitality needs expression. Therefore, if you say you have reverence for God, the value of your words must be demonstrated with actions.

Now you may be asking yourself—how do I get into inter-dimensional awareness? What should I do? Since meditation may be practiced with eyes open, partially closed, or fully closed, we recommend you choose to have your eyes *open* and use a concentration method. The brain is to be quieted down as a preparation for meditation, yet it will remain poised and alert.

For a simple introductory practice we will use a living tree. Please stop reading until you can actually look at a living one—or at an excellent photograph of one, at least. Do not proceed until this is accomplished.

Now concentrate and focus your attention on the leaves. Notice the shape of the leaves, its spine and veins. These spines and veins are used to help all the surface receive nourishment. If there is fruit on the tree you observe, notice the way the fruit is attached and grows. If you are in a blossom season, notice the blossom. Notice the sunlight on the leaves. Some night you can also observe the moonlight on the leaves as they sleep. Now look through the spaces of the leaves and branches and see the sky beyond. The sky is cosmic space and not far away. *You* are in it; the tree is in it.

Guide your concentration into seeing the tree as both an object of beauty and as an intricate, functional design. Perhaps you have some knowledge about photosynthesis and the carbon dioxide/oxygen process? Then be fully cognizant of the process wherein the plants and trees take your breath's waste products and recycle them. This process is only one of the intricate necessities of your life. It is a process that is complex in its many levels and connections because nothing on the planet stands apart or alone. You would die without the trees and plants, as would the animals and birds. And the number of trees and plants must be in numerical balance with your populations. You are cutting down the trees while increasing the population. This is causing a gigantic imbalance. Do you want to wear gas masks and live under artificial domes by this century's end as a punishment (effect) for your ignorance (cause)? Truly are you headed in that direction.

The more you learn about botany, biology, zoology and the natural sciences, the more appreciation your open-eyed meditations will contain until one day you become a walking meditation in communion with God through nature. Then your presence will be holy and your actions of love and support will be a result of your acknowledged dominion or responsibility. When you assume responsibility you can join in that shared conversation from one living thing to another and fulfill divinity's union.

For now, your deep caring may cause pain as you see how pollution is harming the air that you breathe. And you will want to stop the ozone layer destruction because the ozone keeps those powerful ultra-violet rays from harming humans, animals and plants. Do you recognize that the dehydration of the plants will happen more quickly without a protective ozone layer? How can you keep enough fresh, necessary drinking water for all lifeforms on land without that ozone shield? Will you and others delay while the air becomes drier and all living things become parched and thirsty for moisture?

Some earth research is incorrectly purporting that humans need only a certain number of inches of plant life to sustain your breath on a monthly or annual basis. However, we point out that this figure works only in theory since your air is polluted, and clean air is a vital factor in establishing and retaining balance. The more air you pollute the more green growth you need—not less. The rapid acceleration of your technology and industrialization, which uses "natural" air sources quickly, without rapid replenishment, is causing a serious imbalance in the oxygenation process.

Be concerned that the cycles involving checks and balances are being thrown off, and move to restore correct balance immediately. As the subtle changes within the air and water (including salt water) occur, danger zones are not always discernible until you reach a critical level. It is important for you to realize that although it is invisible to you, negative change is occurring. At this current date and in your present stage of industrialization positive action is urgent.

There are chemicals that "eat" the atmosphere around you. Fluorocarbon is one of the worst culprits. These chemicals are causing disease in many oxygen-producing trees. In other places you are cutting down trees at an extreme rate. The carbon dioxide/oxygen process of photosynthesis is quickly going into overload. As mentioned, if the destructive pace continues at its present rate, you will need physical domes to live within by the end of the century for environmental protection and the carbon dioxide/oxygen exchange support.

To bring the intra-dimensional aspect of awareness back into focus, note with great regard that all "natural" things that give and sustain life need to be kept in balance. The allowable variance factor is only 2%. When a 7% adverse change is reached, you bring extreme changes on yourselves and all of life. Since these changes occur in a cyclical or linking fashion, *you dare not effect or drastically change the natural function of anything.* Therefore, see yourself as part of the intra-dimensional life on your planet, and take care of it. To say you are enlightened or caring without grasping this expanded understanding and acting on it is a lie.

To know if you are being reverent to God, then, and thus experiencing true worship, you need to be open to the life-giving energy from beyond your physical plane of existence plus care for all that is considered natural. As you cherish all lifeforms and the physical planet—truly wanting their continued existence and full potential expression—you are demonstrating true worship. Be harmless. Be helpful. Be genuinely human and responsive to guidelines for life. Utilize free will, free choice constructively.

The spiritual human relates to the soul. Your spiritual aspect is perceptual and has both an earth and a cosmic reality. Spirituality is perceptual analysis of what the soul is seeing or sensing. This perception can be narrow, broad, limited or unlimited. It can be limited to the area just within the electrical field of the individual's body, or it can be as broad as the universe. It can soar beyond the planet's surface, comprehend the solar system and see the galaxy as part of a universe. The true spiritual person is inter-dimensional.

Inter-dimensional awareness, then, is the avenue by which you humans contact and express God's essence. Since your soul resides in a physical container, it can perceive both body and planetary physicalness within this area's locale. Yet it can extend beyond this level into the additional perception of the dimensions beyond this 3rd dimensional world. The soul is the one who sees and communicates with all beings outside of the physicalness of earth, yet it must communicate through the body container's brain.

The brain's inherent ability to be inter-dimensional is not presently utilized by most of humanity due to lack of use and a shifted awareness. However, when using this ability fully the soul has absolute capabilities that allow it to interrelate with all existence. It can realize the responsibility within its physical existence in relationship to all things that exist, animate and inanimate, visible and invisible. Inter-dimensional awareness, for instance, allows you to perceive my reality and the angelic realms in their many classifications. It allows you to perceive that God does exist and you, as the soul, exist beyond your physical body. Hence, you can understand the eternal aspect of life.

There are lifeforms that have intelligence and life energy but not souls. (See the book Cosmic Revelation.) Your cells and photoplasma constantly receive electrical charges from cosmic energy. The "thing" that brings together intention, brain, all senses and bodily functions is the soul energy that pulsates within you. As you focus attention to that soul energy with a willingness for progressive changes, it says yes and gives you more energy. The soul energy "wattage," or glow, also increases with use. The more you use it, the happier the soul is.

This soul energy is, of course, removable from its container, the body. It is multi-dimensional in its ability to move, perceive and exist. The 3rd dimensional denseness of the physical form is not its reality.

The air in a room is the same as the air outside the room once the walls are removed (unless it is polluted). Pause a moment now and look out the window. Sense the inter-dimensional understanding of existence beyond this planet.

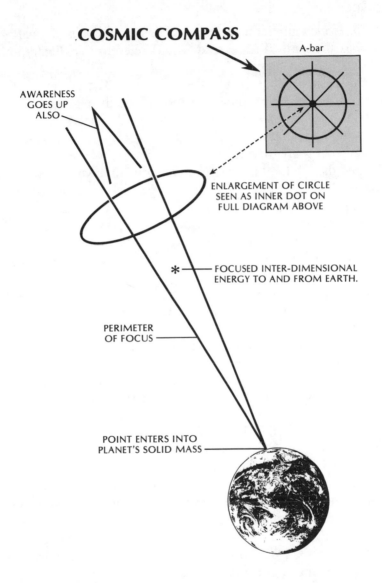

COSMIC COMPASS

A-bar

AWARENESS GOES UP ALSO

ENLARGEMENT OF CIRCLE SEEN AS INNER DOT ON FULL DIAGRAM ABOVE

FOCUSED INTER-DIMENSIONAL ENERGY TO AND FROM EARTH.

PERIMETER OF FOCUS

POINT ENTERS INTO PLANET'S SOLID MASS

103

The following information explains how focused energy reaches the earth. Please read it and refer to the illustration "The Cosmic Compass."

The cosmic compass is called an A-bar. The center of the A-bar is the circle as shown in the enlarged diagram.

Inter-dimensional awareness is directed toward the earth from any or all levels downward. You, in turn, are able to perceive upward through the same energy to the 7th level. Beyond the 7th level it is necessary to fine tune your focus. As you go higher in awareness, it is necessary to have concentrated focus until you reach a point where you are *in* awareness. At that point is a true sense of knowingness and inner peacefulness. The top level of the upward-focused energy then is totally in Universal Mind and you have a sense of being close to God.

There are 12 parts to the compass: an outer circle, eight energy beams (arms), one inner circle and the needle, which is the focused energy. The point of the needle goes into the earth's solid mass, so the planet itself is aware of the energy.

The purpose of the cosmic compass diagram is to help you understand how an individual can have an awareness of spiritual beings, God, and the special vibration that is focused on earth.

Using the concept that God is at level 24 and the Great Rays are at level 22, please perceive that they can direct an idea or a focused energy to the planet's surface at will.

Under an edict or instruction from level 24 or 22—perhaps both—other beings such as archangels may also feed ideas into that focused energy. This focused energy may be directed to a specific place, person or object. The contact "point" opens up the door of perception for inter-dimensional awareness and allows you to see back out into that higher realm.

104

The arms of the compass are meridians carrying the energy into a broader field. Often this A-bar is used within a larger A-bar to reach a definite point on the planet.

Focused inter-dimensional energy is not in itself cosmic energy. It is the vitality of the intention contained in electrical current that energizes the cosmic energy. Thus it uses cosmic energy to carry the intention to the specific area.

Special energy is generated when a being or a group of beings has a specific intention that is to be directed to the planet and its inhabitants.

Each being, even the Silver Ray, starts out using a larger A-bar on a true universal level, then within that A-bar goes to a smaller one to find a quadrant, then a smaller one within the previous A-bar to find a planet and/or a region.

Electrical energy, radio, TV and microwave energies are also examples of this invisible inter-dimensional force. This force that seems to be multi-faceted, with different qualities or characteristics, is really one force called cosmic energy with a myriad of applications.

Your creative soul spark can be traced backwards to God and this energy. Since energy continues, its permanent spark is still within your physical lifeform or dense body substance. This God-spark *still* contains cosmic energy even when removed from its "home" or dense body structure. Be assured your true soul identity knows no death!

A section of the brain not being utilized by humans at this time knows and understands inter-dimensional perceptions. In fact, this understanding is built into your body. You are already equipped and just need to get it operant again. By relying on your own capabilities as a sensory physical person, the perception has become dormant from lack of use. To begin its awakening process, use the tree/leaf exercise given earlier.

105

Shall I expand on this? Inter-dimensional ability is inherent in each person although not utilized at this time. You have on your planet those clairvoyants who have the ability to see energies behind or beyond physical density. You normally call these invisible, but some can see into the 4th dimensional levels and witness either spiritual forms or some of us angelic beings. Development of this capability does not make a person a saint necessarily; it is only a fine tuning of an inhibited ability dormant within each person. In acknowledging this as "normal" you will open to its development.

Should you wish to develop this inherent ability, the procedure requires slowing down the brain's mental activity so that you are aware of your physical body *beyond your breath*. You need to feel the *functioning of your heartbeat and also hear it*. Then when you are aware of only the heartbeat's feel and sound, begin to resonate that heartbeat with the rhythm of all that is around you. When you become still the senses experience a message from the united heart and soul.

The heartbeat tunes into everything around it, and it becomes a pulsing resonance with life. There is a unity in the beat. There is a unity in the vibration. I have said it before, but this heart-listening experience will let you experience a whole new world. *All life is synchronized in its existence.* (That is why we insist you cease playing with hydrogen, nuclear and atomic substance until you have soul integrity and intention to use energy properly.)

Every thought put forth (cause) comes back (effect) and is contained within this planet; therefore, all the thoughts, energies and thrusts of peace are to be brought into a single focused and synchronized moment. Your heart and soul can feel peace, whereas your intellect cannot, because the brain has a different function. This information was given in your biblical reports of long ago.

106

This soul/heart perception of inter-dimensional reverence is an expansion of a deep inner-core knowing, a love of God, creation and life. Use your eyes to see and your heart to hear and feel, thus experiencing purity in your worship. It is no accident that your heart is the key to worship, for the actual energy battery, your soul, sits beside it in your human body chest. The soul's consciousness moves about in the many dimensions even as you listen to the rhythms and cycles of life in the physical with your heart. You are a marvelous creation. Do not destroy this opportunity to begin a full experience and expression of it.

Throughout your civilizations there have been special people who you have considered great ones or holy persons. We of the angelic realm have worked with them many times. Those you call spiritual masters have walked this earth and learned to express soul/body balance even as you are doing. A master is *not* to be revered, even though he or she is enlightened; however, a master is to be greatly respected when attending you as a teacher and guide during this Time of Awakening.

Because these masters have had bodies in past times during lives on earth, they well understand human behavior, perhaps better than I can, yet all of us have a role in this present task. These enlightened ones have assisted humanity over many eons of time even while your consciousness was at its lowest ebb. They were the great prophets and teachers and models of righteousness who kept God-realization alive and hope ever-present in the most desolate of times and places. I honor those masters as we speak now about their gifts to earth.

Onto the planet each of the great ones came with a deep soul desire to heal a wounded earth and its negative population. They came from a true soul desire to free their sleeping compatriots from a long extended misadventure and shepherd them back from atrophy into blossoming God-expression.

They came like dew drops of love, each glistening in rainbow brilliance amidst the dark night of human souls.

Their presence was often ignored, unappreciated, even challenged by evil and pain. Sometimes physical murder was the final tribute to that persistence. Why did they persist? They knew something you, too, must learn and express to the fullest. *Love heals all things.*

Some expressed this from their deep philosophical wisdom. Others gave simple and loving guidelines of immense emotional impact. They come into all cultures in all earth time periods, especially when most needed and called for.

Sometimes angels attended them or brought support to keep love's lamp alive and peace a coherent choice. As I have been told by Archangel Michael, Gabriel, and Raphael particularly, belief was kept alive throughout the desolate detour of humanity's inequity by these earth leaders who believed you were only the sleeping Christ. These masters had something each of you needs so desperately right now, *faith . . . faith . . . faith.* Each master believed with unshakable certainty in God's plan for wisdom and love to be balanced and brought together in a glorious physical union on this planet, in this solar system and in this galaxy. Without that enduring persistence and commitment to you, your history might not stand as an open door to this great moment of your awakening. Spiritual teachers of all times and places have respected, loved and believed in you. Please do no less! For even we of the angelic realms come to call you forward to that soul recollection of beauty and harmony that you are. Now kindly pause again here and quiet your mind. Feel the thumping of your heart.

Attune your heartbeat to the rhythm of the planet and all those around it such as Lord Jesus, Buddha, Krishna and the many others who have served you with the deepest caring. Feel their compassion and certainty that you are a beloved creation, that you are a wise and loving soul worthy to host the presence of God's consciousness.
Feel it.
Know it.
Put the book down awhile and be still.
Be still and know you are the light evermore.

★ ★ ★ ★ ★ ★ ★ ★ ★ ★ ★ ★

As we resume our sharing, I wish to clarify several methods used by your great masters and Lords to arouse earth's sleeping souls. Many different beings have been involved in the rehabilitation and resurrection of humanity and earth, but you are the ones, now, to expand our foundation of wisdom and love. You have the energy of God and the Great Rays to accelerate the Christ consciousness within you to achieve planetary peace.

Just as in the past, communication from spiritual and angelic realms is possible. Prophecy, vision, dreams, prayer, meditation, contemplation, nature's beauty, music's refreshment, art's glory, laughter and joy and love are your helpmates in this growth and expansion event we plan. Use them with discernment, power and clarity until one day we shall have no further need to use words at all and shall be together in quietude beyond silence. But let us speak of your present possible contacts with spirit in a closer focus and examination.

Prophecy: Prophecy is a message sent from higher spiritual influences to elicit positive behavior changes from earth's inhabitants. Since these messages of prophecy require an individual messenger or messengers to receive them, the word *prophet* is used. A prophet, as recorded in your earth's past historical documents, can be of two types.

The first category utilizes channeling or the receiving of information via visions, dreams, telepathic contact, or some combination thereof.

Visions: A vision is a profound sensory experience that may or may not include telepathy. It is a very powerful moment *experienced in the body with great emotional impact*. This enormous energy experience is seldom if ever forgotten by the few humans who have it. Those who have visions hold their memory as jewels in their conscious memory. These are usually received with tremendous urgency for action either in their own lives or for others.

Dreams: A dream message occurs during a bodily state of rest or sleep and is a special kind of vision, less sensory (body experience) and more telepathic (mental) within the brain itself. This message can be a cleansing for emotional purposes or so graphic in its intense presentation of details that the one experiencing it believes it has a reality that may even occur.

Telepathy: Telepathy is mental communication using thought energy to send or receive a message. When you on earth receive telepathic communications from our realm, you usually experience a picture, a "light packet" with accompanying explanation and highlights that seem auditory . . . or simply a great knowingness centered within the brain. This communication does not require the sleep stage as dreams do. It normally occurs in what you call an altered state such as meditation, contemplation, prayer, or quiet times.

110

Superior or pure telepathy occurs when the individual places *no personality perception* on the information as it is received and only later uses analysis and discernment in examining its pure content. Today, because so much information is being sent to so many people, there are extreme variances in the purity of messages due to personality interference and interpretation of our intent.

The second major form of prophecy occurs when (in very rare instances only!) an enlightened spiritual master returns to earth with a primary purpose of being a prophet. From birth, or later on in life, such an individual is able to maintain an intensified energy field of great wisdom and therefore to relate information to others with inordinate clarity. Many religious teachings of historical time periods on earth have centered on the teachings of such individuals.

Finally, on very rare occasions, angelic beings have appeared to certain individuals to state a message that is of immediate importance to that individual or to many people. Our experience with this method has been quite difficult because the person may either label the experience as insanity or deny it totally. When our contact brings forth a positive response and action, individual or group members of society may resist or retaliate. There may be those who accuse the recipient of falsehood or blasphemy. We do not wish any further witch burnings, possibly caused by some of our angelic messages, to ever occur again in human history.

There are many instances of angelic contacts and prophets in your biblical teachings. Even in more current times there are messages of import such as the event when Mother Mary's energy appeared bringing information to small children who are innocent and would not be considered crazy.

If a form of worship, church, institution or mode of religious conduct generates from any of the kinds of prophecy

111

mentioned above we ask you to realize this reaction has been created by humans from your dimension. The interpretations are from your own perceptions. We have never told humans to start religions.

On the contrary, our observation is that the instituting of many individual religions has separated human from human rather than connecting all humans to God and planetary peace. There is a common thread of love and peace to life that we hope you will see and truly apply from whatever information we bring you in the Time of Awakening. True free will in worship with spiritual application or action is the challenge of your civilizations.

We have asked you to care for the planet and all life on it, and to revere God above all else. Still, all of your churches, your religious rituals and beliefs have *not* established and maintained the peace we require of you. Then what can be done? We will not ask you to cease all current religious practices, but we do request sincere evaluation of present spiritual attitudes and applications. What can be adapted in your life to totally focus power for peaceful living?

Will you change if need be?

How? For, as mentioned, you have a planetary obligation to establish peace, and there is no exception to this.

Spiritual values are your foundation stones for peace. All of you who say you believe must now express your belief. Hear me well. If those who say they love God and wish for peace would practice it, we could quickly mobilize about ⅓ of the planet's population to a strongly focused intention. That would give the impetus you need and establish a basis of enormous advantage!

Although thought has the potential to bring about positive change, it can also cause conflict in many people because they have acquired a resistance to change. The process of habituation and improper use of free will have been the nemesis of your planet. The principle of the "Hundredth Monkey," as you will call it, can work because the thought of any individual or animal *does* go out into local, global consciousness. And it can even go beyond into the ethers of Universal Mind, as well. *All* lifeforms then have the possibility of using this same idea or thought at either one of these levels.

As a human or animal uses the thought, beneficially or negatively, others can notice the resulting action, choose to use that same idea, or behave differently. It is *not* true that all humans or animals get the same thought, however. Most behavior is learned or modeled. As the very first monkey accessed the idea of washed potatoes from Universal Mind and behaved in a new way, an affirmative thought was sent back out into global consciousness. Any other monkey could receive that idea even at a different location because this thought was vibrating on an established animal frequency that all monkeys could utilize. (The animal frequency, incidentally, is actually different from your human frequency.) If the second monkey was in close proximity, it could follow, or directly model, the action of the first monkey and notice how washing the sand off a yam improved the taste.

A monkey on a far away island obviously could not use direct modeling but could use the thought that was contained in global consciousness to replicate monkey number one or monkey number two's behavior. We point out the wonderful opportunity this represents, yet how many other monkeys changed their actions because of the idea or the modeled behavior? Regrettably the majority did *nothing!*

This example shows only part of the problem you humans face because as some individuals are thinking *positive* thoughts, other individuals are thinking *negative* thoughts.

The monkeys who did not respond were merely unconscious; they were not *resisting* the idea of washed food. Your global consciousness contains both polarities, so resistance is there. If the number of each group is the same, no change can take place. The group or persons that put *action* with the thinking, however, put energy for movement behind the thinking and *push* the thought out further and with more force. It is more indelible and influential, so to speak.

If you think a positive peace thought while seated, but then get up and do other actions unrelated to your peace thought, those other actions also have thoughts behind and with them. Therefore, you immediately weaken the prior positive peace thought by not completing its intent before going on to something else.

By virtue of ratios, then, your planetary population needs billions of peace helpers to dramatically maintain any serious change to peace through activities. You cannot manifest your thought desire(s) without action.

If you go to your automobile, open the door, get in and sit and think about starting the vehicle, nothing happens. It is through the *action* of inserting the key, turning it and actively driving the car away that the electrical *connection* is utilized.

Energy is aliveness. Lack of energy is physical demise. The use of energy constitutes action. *Action is life expressing*. We need your peaceful thoughts, of course, but in isolation they are much less valuable than ideas put into action.

Think peace, of course. This is step one. Then go beyond thinking to implementation. It is to both aspects of this peace process that you are now being called. Please accept this clarion call so vital and almost beyond my words to describe.

WORSHIP IN OTHER PLACES WITHIN THE GALAXY

Because examining other options and possible solutions can be helpful, let me share one galactic example of worship that is working well in your universe. In fact, it has resisted *all* negativity since its origin. Purely in the attitude of exploration, I will comment on this area's life patterns that are already known to some of you. I refer to your cousins, the Pleiadians.

For them, reverence has become a state of all-knowingness or acceptance of the Creator as justice, equality, peace, balance and harmony. Their lives are a model of poetically rhythmic group behavior containing concern for their planet and all life on it. They do not kill with thoughts or deeds.

Because true reverence is seldom experienced on earth due to massive spiritual ignorance and abuse, and the innumerable rituals that the separate religions have instituted, you must improve. Thus we share the Pleiadian process with you only as an example that purity of reverence was chosen and maintained by nearly every individual.

In the Pleiades, individuals establish and continue their God-feeling of connection in this way. First, within each home dwelling the individual (and also the spiritual community in which they associate) selects times of peaceful contemplation. Second, they have created exquisite dome-shaped spiritual buildings with an interior of concentrated rainbow light where many people can attend simultaneously. Third, they also are able to feel the God presence outside of any structure in what you would call nature. In other words, regardless of the person's physical location they have three ways that meditation or contemplation can occur in a positive way.

How do they do this? They merely become still within the personality thus quieting the electrical field around them.

115

They also call all lifeforms "friend" and will join openly in any group experience for spiritual devotion. This inner and outer alignment of quietude allows soul awareness to lift beyond any external physical objects and become part of Universal Mind. Here, true awareness energizes the individual and helps maintain a certainty that all existence, including their own, is safely contained within cosmic energy.

There is much more to it than this, of course. It is the quiet and scrupulous commitment to purity, group caring and reverence for God, however, that is the Pleiadian hallmark. I have noted they are never without God (or good) in their activities. We wish for you the same! I suggest you contemplate this information only if it feels appropriate to do so. I do not offer it as your solution, simply an example. The powerful Pleiadian relationship to God and their continuing state of reverence has allowed them to withstand all negativity ever brought to the consciousness of that region. I gather this was a major reason why Archangel Michael recruited volunteers from that region long ago when your planet was ready for caretaking.

On your planet with its huge population, reverence for God and willingness to follow local rules of conduct and laws, in an orderly manner, are requisite. On other planet systems where all creations truly revere the Bringer-of-all-life without question, legal regulations are infrequent, and spiritual know-ingness prevails. Where the will of the little self is so misused, as it presently is on earth, guidelines, rules and laws become quite necessary. I merely point this information out for clarity and some continuity.

We notice that if one person kills another on earth, you have many explanations about the level of deliberate murderous intention. Your courts examine various "extenuating" circumstances and the consequential punishment that should ensue. In your prayers you ask us for advice about capital punishment and the consequences of murder as a religious matter.

You must understand that in the human intelligence there is that moment of knowingness when a decision to kill is made. The individual actually makes the decision to take another's life. It is only an instant in your perception, perhaps, yet it is a decision. There is *no action* that is not decided within the intelligence. Even those who are being attacked must decide to defend themselves, and they are usually excused, which is appropriate for the most part.

Your most interesting excuse for murder is insanity. Insanity is a multiplicity of thoughts wanting expression or action at the same time. Instead of focusing on one activity and finishing its sequence of thinking and actions, the brain draws into it many thoughts at one time. Hence, it becomes confused. Now you must remember that whatever is occurring in the thought process is actually sending out messages to the senses and physical body for action. If the person is thinking five thoughts, even if they are incomplete, the intelligence is working with five ideas at one time. Messages of action, or conduct to go with those five ideas, are being sent to the rest of the machine at the same instant. Insanity is a short-circuiting of the thought process because there is no stable thought or concept to rely on. May I remind you that the peaceful and innocent do not have mental confusion.

Nonetheless, when a person takes the life energy of another, there is within the entire complexity of the human an *all-knowing moment*. Regardless of what confusion is going on within the intelligence, there is a moment when eternity seems to stop. In that moment the individual decides whether or not it will continue with the action. *There is the ability within each individual to abort destructiveness*. Even the

117

instantaneous decision to follow through with the destruction of another person occurs with, and by, choice.

Why?

This deterrent to violence is built into the intelligence, the brain and the soul, so that there would *never* be an excuse for murderous attack. Murder is always done with knowledge, and the deliberate removal of human life is very serious because life is an expression of God.

I, and many, have come to help you maintain life and avoid immense disaster. You are engaging in thoughts and deeds that could lead to catastrophic mass suicide and murder. Will you then say to us, "We were insane?"

If the planet is seriously damaged or destroyed, will you say, "We were insane," and ask to be forgiven? Evil is an unrestrained negative thought or deed. In your perception you call it insanity. Please ponder this issue carefully. You have been granted grace by your Lord Jesus for past events. For this life, however, you will have an evaluation, be assured.

On your planet now, and throughout the histories of most of your civilizations, you have had warfare. This warfare currently exists, as I have no need to belabor. You may wonder how a spiritual being in a physical body can continue living in this framework of warfare with any joy. My reply is that things are rapidly and positively changing. Persevere boldly and be part of a wondrous solution!

Another question frequently asked is, "Can you defend yourself if someone tries to attack you?" The answer has two parts. The first part is, "Yes, you may defend yourself at the moment of attack, assuming you have not sought to overcome another first."

Secondly, if you have defended yourself in the moment, you must immediately become peaceful and return to positive

118

conduct. You do not prepare for domination in, or continuance of, this aggressive action. Through healed attitudes you must live in harmony. The need for domination and control must be eliminated since all of the processes of war emanate from the thought patterns of hate, greed, avarice, pride and so on. These are the negatives that hold you in their power. Only a bold and imaginative soul intuition will free humanity from a likelihood of continuing planetary madness.

At this point in our discussion it may seem to some humans that I have been stern. If so, please grasp that this message is not only for those who already seek peace, but for the general population who now are being called to serve. All of you are needed. Work together, please, and let peace flourish. If you are reading this material you are likely striving to grow and learn. This striving or seeking needs to be acknowledged and I do acknowledge you. I acknowledge you as a soul. I acknowledge you as an energized human being wanting to bring the two aspects of soul and body reality together.

Yes, your planet is in danger, but you have a magnificent spiritual realm working with you, and our support is incredibly powerful! Our group is made up of many different energies, each having the ability to assist in a variety of ways. Some of us can work with your intelligence; some can work with your emotions and feelings. If needed, some can give you technological data. Some will give you information to help you with your spiritual awareness. All of this help comes freely forward to assist you in fulfilling your responsibility as souls on earth.

As the Time of Awakening progresses and your illumination accelerates, the balloon of false teaching will burst. The motion of truth will shake humanity's rituals and godless substitutes until The Source is seen as the reality of all existence and its qualities are finally brought forth in pervasive expression.

We assist you so that as a soul expression you become a bright, luminous joy to behold.

Knowing that *we* and you are in harmonic concert gives us additional vitality to move faster and work harder. So rejoice in who you are. Rejoice in the fact that you are reading this document. Rejoice that you are seeking. Rejoice in the advancement that is beginning to occur. And as you look upward to behold the majesty of the cosmos, also look at the planet and your fellow humans to behold the beauty of God's creation here. All plans are progressing because of you. Things are moving to that point of fuller understanding and expression of harmonious living called the Time of Radiance.

Many humans have been cemented in spiritual error, particularly some of the most intelligent ones. Captured by externals and material substitutions for the simplicity of peaceful God-awareness, they have not used God's influence to reclaim a prodigal planet. Please consider what has been presented in this document. IN A TRULY REVERENT STATE THE SOUL HAS NO RITUALS, ONLY AWARENESS. Awareness is the basis of worship. Only its lightning thrust can fuse a connection between heaven and earth into a permanent reality capable of healing this ailing planet and its people.

As the beauty of the physical world becomes more evident to you and the music of the spheres seeps into your awareness, *hear* the birds as they sing to the trees, the flowers and to you. Let your heart beat with the beauty of *life* as it gathers its momentum for continuance of the planet safety for all of its inhabitants. Let there be Preservation of all Life— Peace on Earth! Rejoice at this awakening that opens your eyes so that you *see* and *understand* the cycles of all life. As you begin to expand your awareness, you will gain the true understanding of inter-dimensional perception. You will also understand the multi-leveled word *love*, for this word contains the essence of caring for all life and its many forms.

Go forward then, residents of earth, toward new understandings that encompass *all* knowledge as it is seen with the eyes of those having inter-dimensional awareness.

Your soul is wise and can renew its majesty in a moment. It has had many learning chapters here on planet earth, so you could have both intra (same level) and inter-dimensional (higher level) knowledge. Isn't it time to bring them together in a mighty exclamation for physical world peace?

Say yes and we will flow with you, bringing heaven into earth, earth into heaven.

Join with us so that doves may truly inherit the earth and transform an ailing planet's destiny.

121

Chapter VI

Time

Constantly in your conversations you use the word *time*. At both a subconscious and conscious level you are very much aware of time and its measurement into linear segments. We hear you say over and over again, "I do not have enough time."

You, as the human civilization, have devised various tools and methods of measuring this time. You have had both elaborate mechanisms and very simple ones such as sundials, lunar clocks, and water clocks. Today you use quartz digital timepieces for even greater accuracy. Within each of these mechanical devices for time measurement is a physically delineated motion (a cause and effect) that registers a result such as hours, minutes and seconds.

Your calendars continue this count with divisions into days, weeks, months and years. Then, by some earth agreement you jiggle time around in physical travel so that you lose or gain it. You move it up an hour or back an hour, depending on the seasons, so that today the hands on your dials move in a ceaseless march that binds you to a linear definition of life. You are born, live and die by the clock in technological societies, whereas in more natural environments you live and die by the rhythms and cycles of earth and stars. These little time blocks seem to give you structure and control over events

123

and circumstances of earthly existence, but they also establish the concept of past, present and future in some very limiting ways.

Since past, present and future are terms you use to specify parts of a greater whole, how do I, Uriel, help you when I do not have time in my dimension? Rather than time we angels have events and experiences.

An event is a series of actions that result in a specific conclusion. This is another way of stating cause and effect. When the series of actions is over for that event, it is immediately in the past. *Future events depend on present actions or thoughts. They are probable and cannot be predicted with certainty.*

Time should have no power over you; it is not a real thing. Events are actual experiences and have no substitutes. As mentioned, we have events and experiences in our realms, and these have both cause and effect. What you call the ''passing of time'' does not exist for us. In fact, because of its deception and limitation, only on your planet, and one other, does linear time measurement even exist.

Time does not explain the specific conclusion created by an action, for instance. To us an event is a potential thought field or unstructured energy until its action is finished. At our level in the collective memory of all events in the omniverse, which is called Universal Mind, there are records of *completed* events. Moreover, these records are constantly being updated or revised by all new events, from all sources, ever-expanding that collective memory of Universal Mind.

Since Universal Mind is the totality of all consciousness, or *completed events* (much like your computer input), THE FUTURE IS NOT YET REGISTERED THERE! *The future is a potential state dependent on past and present action.*

Nowhere on earth is the future already established and determined by what you call fate or God.

If the future were already known, free will and free choice could not exist, and incarnation would have no meaning. In a very real sense there would be no need for life or consciousness to express itself. Therefore, any teaching that suggests fatalism or the idea that past, present and future is simultaneously experienced is invalid. I do not mean that strong trends and likelihoods are unreal; we are here on earth because negative probabilities are very real! However, they are not absolute. Cosmic energy is unmanifested reality awaiting pregnancy and birth. Your future is only *probable*, not already defined and established.

Growth, expansion and continuing opportunity for development are the very foundation of God consciousness. Ask in meditation if this statement is the truth for you. Explore. Be unlimited.

By relinquishing misperceptions regarding the linear nature of time you will be truly free to expand beyond your limitations and confusions. We are penetrating this misconception of time with a great spiritual impulse so you can truly understand your place in this solar system and galaxy.

Since you are so dependent on the concept of time, it is important that we refrain from totally "doing away" with it. Therefore we use your concept of time by advising you that this is the Time of Awakening. It is to be an experience! a series of events. Within the Time of Awakening was the Time of Transformation, and now you are experiencing the Time of Change and the Time of the Dove. Also during this time period will be the gleaning time. Ultimately these "times," or events and experiences, will lead into that enlightened period called the Time of Radiance. This is our intention. The exact date is probable, yet the event will come from our insistence.

Let us explore your concept of time more clearly. Humanity developed time to help you count or identify the rising of the sun and the arrival of the moon at any given place on the planet.

When your space travellers go up from the earth, except for their clocks there is NO AWARENESS of time, only of events. Can you grasp that? If you get beyond the thoughts or electrical field of your globe, you quickly lose the perception of time. You can also forget time while living on the planet, but it is more difficult in noisy cities and large metropolitan areas than in rural country quietude.

In music you have a whole note, a half-note, a quarter note, then faster to an eighth, a sixteenth and so forth. This musical rhythm is merely an experience to present an idea of fast and slow cycles. The Silver Ray wants you to be aware of the rhythm of your existence, including the sun and moon cycles certainly, as well as the seasons and all of nature. Just as the planets, stars, galaxies and universe all have their cycles, so do you on earth.

When all goes well for you, and within you, you have a sense of harmony. When there is a disruption, you sense disharmony, as if something were wrong, but you cannot always discern the difficulty.

Universal law requires harmony. All matter has its place of existence, its place of movement, its rhythm. Our concern regarding your hydrogen and nuclear testings and possible use of these lawless creations and horrendous devices is that they can greatly disrupt both planetary and galactic harmonies.

The plan for humanity's survival does not allow for abrupt change on this planet, or elsewhere for that matter. And what occurs in one area can adversely change adjoining regions. So stay with that divinely created cycle! It is there with good reason.

Now let us imagine this scene for a few moments.

It is nighttime. Stars are shining in abundance, like jewels against a dark cloth. The moon is a quarter visible to you. You look at the sky and begin to feel peaceful. Then you go to rest and sleep peacefully.

Without a clock you awaken in the morning. Perhaps you wonder what time it is before realizing it doesn't really matter. You feel so peaceful that you do not want to go out into "the world."

Your food tastes better. People with whom you come in contact during the day greet you pleasantly, difficulties are handled without stress, and you are patient. Do you notice the ingredient in this scene? It is the absence of pressure caused by time measurement. This does not mean that your events and experiences are not happening; it merely means that you are choosing not to label or confine them. *The pressure and anxiety of your society and/or civilization is caused by time*, and in some cases, by attempting to be over-active with unimportant tasks. This preoccupation leads to fragmentation and a sense of anxiety.

How often have you said, "I have to get this done" when it wasn't really critical? How many occasions have you established deadlines at home or work that were not urgent?

Earth has a due date to create peaceful existence; therefore, within your present time measurement let peace be your personal and planetary deadline.

Talk to a farmer and you will hear about the crops, the soil, the weather, and a sense of the season as it relates to climate. Talk to a tribesperson in Africa or Australia, and there will be no comment that it is 2:00 P.M. on Wednesday, February

15th. Events transpire and activity and actions happen, to be sure. Each thing, animate and inanimate, has its cycle of existence, and development. You may call the cycle growth; we call it development. It contains three possible cycles: forward pulsation, maintaining pulsation or reverse pulsation. The forward pulsation is a plus (+) factor, and the reverse pulsation is a minus (−) factor. A maintenance or equilibrium cycle would be symbolized as (+ +). Everything through built-in electrical energy can simultaneously act and monitor itself.

The gravitational pull/push from your planet constantly gives off plus pulses (+ + +) to energize each matter form. This current from the earth itself energizes *all life*. This energy current is the reason you feel good walking out-of-doors when the air is clear. Springtime feels particularly invigorating to you because the pulses are pushing outward most abundantly and are evident everywhere. On a galactic scanner they would be seen as sparks of blue-white pulsating energy.

When you feel ''good'' or are full of vitality, you may be in an area of abundant plus activity. Bodies of water are especially energized because water conducts energy, and its molecular composition allows energy to flow freely.

What you are now calling ''ions'' is another name for these plus activities. Pluses come *from* the earth. The planet itself is a giant battery that stores these pluses in its center and sends them back out. This recharging process requires heat from the sun.

Areas that are constantly frozen, such as your Arctic and Antarctic regions, are low in vitality and plus activity. You would experience a vitality at first. Then a feeling of depression would ensue as no greenery, rock or plant growth exists to give you a sense of change. Although appearing desolate,

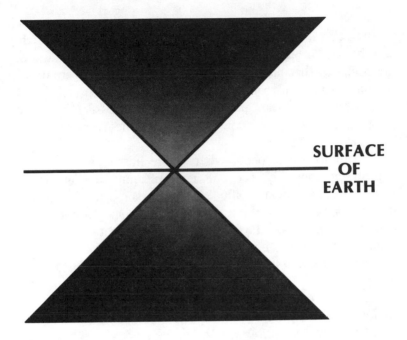

SURFACE OF EARTH

many of your arid areas still have pluses and can be reclaimed. The potential for change exists and requires moisture as the necessary ingredient to initiate that change.

Now that I have described pluses, you may be wondering about the minus factor. Minuses within the land occur when atomic or nuclear molecules have dropped into an area. By absorption, the land begins reclamation in a horizontal band fanning out 2.5 times the size of the original impact area. This band goes north, east, south and west and then downward to reach an apex. If you were to draw it you would have a triangle above the surface and one directly below it. Height and width above the surface is mirrored in the interior of the planet to enable concentrated energized reclamation by the planet itself.

The neutralization of the earth and the purification of the soil then go through a cycle that may take years depending on the rocks in that area. As rocks absorb negative vibrations, the more solid the rock mass is in any area, the quicker will be the healing. Rocks also allow smaller life such as algae, fungi and bacteria to grow and hasten the reversal of the negative impulses.

The minuses also occur where there has been fire, explosion or violence. To accept that all life, animate and inanimate, has an inherent vitality is to understand the formula of the cycles. As stated, three possibilities exist: positive, negative and maintaining. Positive is forward; negative is reverse. When a specific place is struggling, we say it is *maintaining. The environment and the weather may then tip the balance either way.*

All lifeforms interact with electrical current in their surroundings and adjust their molecules or cells to the intensity of this current pulsation pattern or cycle.

(In human body development a minus cycle occurs when the brain pauses in its forward push. Physical development can go into a downward spiral, which means the body will not grow to maturity. Some mental retardation is also caused by downward spiral action.)

Increasingly you will hear people say, "We need to get back into harmony with the land." This is absolutely correct! The primary reason is so that you can begin to fully feel the *vitality* of the planet to let it rejuvenate and heal you, and for you to return that gift of caring and support. There is to be *NO waiting* to the last minute to care for this planet.

It is important that each of you as an individual, and collectively as all humanity, become involved in the issues of planetary concern and preservation of all life *immediately.* A cold heart and uncaring mind must now awaken to wisdom, love and peace or lose what you call a "golden" spiritual opportunity. You must be virtuous. Your lords, masters and teachers of all cultures have spoken about these virtues. They have given no words of encouragement to your use of conquest or domination, murder and war, but they have all taught about caring and respect for others, love, and peace and harmlessness. Now is the time in evolution for each of you to demonstrate what you have learned.

Because time is important to you, we are changing your perception of it so you will quickly get involved in planetary peace issues. This is our primary method of having you notice the required change ahead so you will not wait. We perceive that when there is considerable time, you procrastinate, and the task is left undone or improperly attended to.

Each of you experienced an unusual event in human history on November 17, 1986. On that date your perception, or sense, of time was given a planetary acceleration that has affected all of life. In its first phase, you received a 7% increase. This was raised to 13% in the spring and finally increased to 20% on November 17, 1987, one year later. Think back a moment to those dates. Twenty percent of what you formerly had as time has disappeared. You have a perception of 80% left. We wonder if you have noticed that time is passing more quickly? Have you personally felt rushed, pressured or even exhausted trying to live your usual lifestyle?

You may incredulously ask, "How could time be changed? Is something like this possible?"

Others are asking, "What's happening to me? I feel very peculiar."

Your physical body does not experience time, so we have intervened in your *thought process*. The Great Rays have raised the energy vibration around earth so you now have a higher consciousness. We are not aging your physical body any faster, however. *It is your brain's processing ability that is affected.* Also, your soul is seriously involved in sending you, the personality, a message that it is time to make changes for peace. Even those light workers who already have a close relationship between soul and personality can feel an urgency about life, a need to move faster.

For most humans, *this accelerated time perception means that you cannot physically accomplish all of the mental ideas you have.* In fact, your body might be affected if you try to do all the activities generated by increased thought. Why? Because the body cannot move rapidly enough to keep pace. The electrical energy around your physical body and around the planet is so highly energized that your brain processes everything, whether event or thought, much more quickly. When the Silver Ray decided to change the consciousness around this planet so it would have an increased vitality or higher rate of molecular movement, we knew all life would be affected. The dark, negative thought pattern around earth is being pierced now, and a funneling effect of rainbow light is showering down.

The way in which this energy affects you can be shown by analogy. If you have a computer and it is analyzing and processing information at a slower rate than you desire, you install a chip (more power) to increase its speed. This power allows faster processing to occur. Now you, as the individual, have had this happen to you. The energy brought in by this great Silver Ray, working with its twin the Gold Ray, has energized other sub-rays and myself, and all of us together have sped up your thinking ability. Your perception of time is accelerated because you are using your brain more rapidly and are thinking a series of thoughts 20% faster.

132

Your brain reaches a conclusion sooner and sends a message to accomplish results faster. It is, at the same time, already receiving information for the next computation. And with this sense of acceleration you are not physically able to achieve the result of the first computation while it is sending you the second one. Therefore you must *select and prioritize* your projects since you are thinking faster than you can physically accomplish the tasks.

Once your brain does its work, your personhood must physically rush to keep up. That is why you feel out of balance. You cannot stop the energy's inflow. You are at its effect. Of course there are individual differences, but all of you are seeking to balance this new experience.

As stated, when the ideas pour out of your brain you must select, prioritize or systematize their order of completion. Probably you cannot do them all, so please discard the less important and focus seriously on the ones you call vital. Since your consciousness has been changed to help you reach a far higher level of understanding and perception, you must use your 80% remaining time factor more wisely. You cannot abuse your physical body and stay well. You can only move so fast before your body becomes a limitation to accomplish what seems to be additional work. We repeat for emphasis that this inability to keep up with your ideas occurs because the vibration of the energy around the earth is higher than it used to be. It only comes so you will focus on peace.

As the Gold and Silver Rays' intention for peace pierces earth's negativity and arrives closer to the surface of your earth with empowerment, your human awareness is improving. The result is that you are moving more rapidly in consciousness. We call it an ''energy push'' to get you moving. The present rate of this incoming acceleration level will be kept constant approximately 14 to 36 months to assist you in your soul purpose.

Once you understand what is happening you can avoid stress and fatigue plus other feelings of unusual pressure by deliberate meditation and brief quiet times to help you *acknowledge, sort, select* and *act*. This process will help you truly integrate and focus more clearly on planetary needs as priority number one. Although these vibrational changes accelerate the mental process, the spiritually unconscious may not understand this first priority. Then learn yourself and teach others what is happening. Acquire a new awareness of peace, and surrender the lifestyle priorities and activities that most of you had two years ago.

Even with this faster brain activity, most humans can do with slightly less sleep than before. You might equate it to a savings of 45 minutes to one hour in each 24-hour period. So you have gained a small gift of needing less rest even amidst your hurry, especially if you are meditating and breathing properly.

Do not be concerned about aging more rapidly as a result of the vibrational changes, for that definitely does not occur. In fact, the worst effect on your aging has been caused from increasingly negative environmental conditions such as polluted air and water, soil toxicities, improper diet, drug abuses, and so on. The acceleration of time without those adverse factors gives a slightly longer life span and would increase the vitality of the cells, thus changing your food intake and eating habits.

The aging process has nothing to do with time measurement, actually. We reiterate that aging has to do with your mental and emotional attitudes, proper diet and liquids, rest and exercise, care given to the physical body, and the quality of the environment in which it exists. You are actually being given a gift of longer life if you learn to take care of your planet. You will have the opportunity to be healthier and live longer with increased vitality, provided you avoid stress caused by unconsciousness regarding this change and its purposes.

Do not attempt to do as much as before! And you should definitely use a *daily* prayer, meditation or quiet time. Meditation allows you to clearly understand that time does not exist and does not control your life. In the quiet there are no ticking clocks, and you have the peace you deserve.

Now let us share some practical suggestions to help you use this consciousness change beneficially.

1. As an individual you must acquire a new habit of *noticing when your mental activity level is accelerating* at an uncomfortable pace. This attention is necessary and critical because until you notice the increased pace, you will just rush along faster and faster and reach a high stress level very quickly.

2. You must *control the mental pace by frequent, deliberate attention to breathing*. This will allow the body a reprieve or brief rest. Breath is both calming and refreshing and causes your brain wave pattern to change from what you term the beta to an alpha state, if maintained. (In other words, you slow it down.) This effect is scientifically documented, and you may read about it elsewhere if desired.

3. Similarly, *more frequent rest periods* will be inordinately helpful, even if you only sit quietly and close your eyes a few minutes. While closing your physical eyes we recommend you use any mental image that represents peacefulness to you. Perhaps the image of a still, unruffled lake or beautiful pond will be beneficial, or a vision of yourself relaxing high on a mountaintop.

Nature scenes of this type are highly recommended, but use any visualization that brings you peace. Select one and stay with it daily for at least a month. Habitual relaxing sessions, even quite brief, will be immensely valuable in these coming days. Learn to enter quickly into a beneficially altered state of rest and hold it. Very important! Very important to your total well-being.

4. In establishing these short yet calming practices you will probably still need to use *one longer meditation period of 15 to 20 minutes daily.* Here you go beyond time, receive clarity on immediate issues and return to your work from a higher awareness. However, ask for wisdom on any issue during your quiet times only after the brain wave pattern has slowed down and you feel internally calm.

Surrender the stress first, and establish and enjoy the peace before beginning any mental activity. You may use quiet times with inspiring music, beautiful colors, or natural scenery, but whether they are available or not, you must have the mental discipline to create an inner peace. Accept that you probably cannot physically accomplish as much as you could before. When you are relaxed about having less time, you will flow into greater clarity.

5. *You must prioritize all activities in terms of their value to the planet's need for peace.* Then and only then will you feel you have enough time. Prioritizing the few absolute tasks will give surety and comfort. Say to yourself and your loved ones, ''I can't do it all, but I can sort out the absolutely urgent things and accomplish those well.''

We remind you that the first priority on everyone's list is: Preservation of all Life—Peace on Earth. Involve yourself in that cause, and do not let your individual, personal activities draw you off course. The time perception change could be painful unless you willingly and consciously make this shift

136

and appreciate yourself and others for their cooperation in the task at hand. PRIORITIZE. DELETE THE UNIMPORTANT ITEMS. COMPLETE THE ESSENTIALS UNFAILINGLY.

6. Nonetheless, mutual support in your significant relationships can be established. If one of you gets stressful without noticing it, a kind and loving reminder to breathe or become still can be offered by others in your family, by friends or by your colleagues at work. Those with whom you spend the most time can help you, even as you agree to help them.

7. It may take courage, but leaders in large working groups, organizations and conglomerates need to teach these ideas and create healthy patterns for group interactions. A few companies and institutions are already doing this. Now the practice must spread.

Your Lord Jesus has said "Be still," as have all major spiritual teachers. Whether you call this moment a refreshing pause, attunement, or prayer, do some kind of group alignment to settle the mental activity and focus the many minds in a group toward stillness. Then your common focus on any idea will be a team effort on a single issue with less personality dispute. If you are wise enough to love God, focus on that, for your willingness to have spiritual assistance and support gives us permission to share suggestions, to guide you.

This "asking" attunes you to the greatest power and wisdom known in life. Why not use it wherever you are? Your life journey will have much caring, peace and joy when you make it with our aid and with those like yourself who have awakened to planetary concerns and are making a contribution toward preserving this most splendid planet.

137

8. The formation of spiritual communities received impetus in recent years and will increase in novel patterns and practices. Even beyond the various religious or church-established living situations, you will seek to be with those who love God and have the same common purpose or intention you do. For the very sensitive ones, especially, you will long for a bonding of energy to give joy, bring stability, and provide a safe, stable environment. There will be what you term "shared housing" in creative and satisfying patterns not normally part of your heritage. The common pattern of marriage partner and family living, and the usual religiously oriented housing groups can be expanded to other patterns. Living with those of a common spiritual goal will bring the greatest joy and support imaginable.

Such companions will love you abundantly and perhaps offer learning experiences to cleanse and heal any negative qualities you choose to change. When you learn to live harmoniously and practice peace, humanity will be more strengthened than I can say. Truly being together in love establishes innovative models for future expansion and development.

Many books discuss spiritual community ideas, and I recommend them. Still, the knowledge is within you always, is it not? In these days you will see more creative ideas in action than you believed possible. They will bring much learning and happiness. Truly, great excitement is ahead for all who choose it.

One of the effects of this increased vibration that showers your planet is that greater inter-dimensional communication from us to you and you to us is possible. Through history a few humans have had what you call psychic experiences. Because the word "psychic" is established in your language, then, let us speak of these things. Is a foretelling of the future really possible?

Will foretold events always happen, and is being psychic something to be feared?

Please understand that by using the brain's thought process, the soul can be connected to both planetary consciousness and Universal Mind. Psychic impressions regarding *future* events must be interpreted by *deductive* reasoning. As the thought process of the brain uses the higher consciousness information that is available *to all people*, it analyzes facts, current actions and *deduces* future outcome. All such statements are *probabilities!* There are now many more individuals who will have this ability, and there is no magic about it. Those who practice stillness will be able to predict the future with increasing clarity and precision. However, do not announce your deductions and conclusions unless you are willing to label them as deductions and accept the consequences, as some psychics have better reasoning ability than others. Past events and present situations are obviously easier to report with accuracy than potential, future ones.

If you will remember that space is not linear, but curves, you can more accurately understand events that seem to be in the future. The curvature of space means that events contained in the global consciousness of a planet ultimately return to their place of origin. Hence, as an example, an event that occurred in Germany will eventually be seen in the United States as it makes its way around the globe. The energy grid lines above the earth are the means by which these things travel. Causes may be registered as past events, but since the present action may still be unfolding, the future effects cannot be truly determined yet, can they?

139

Within Universal Mind both the past and present thoughts of all peoples are available and can be viewed. But a psychic may "see" only random thoughts of a person or persons as those thoughts float up toward Universal Mind. Since their action is incomplete, any reading or interpretation is imperfect. As I have repeatedly suggested, future events are probable. Those who insist on reading and reporting the memory contents of planetary consciousness or Universal Mind without learning how to do so properly are an unsettling threat to humanity at large. I caution you all to realize that in these days of increased consciousness there will be a great deal of confusion as imperfect information regarding the future is reported as fact . . . by humans who believe they are doing the public a favor. Please test any information with spiritual discernment. Yes, even mine.

Always use spiritual discernment; it is within your soul capability. Weigh information with soul purity and not with the human fear level. These days cross-checking of ideas given by established prophets and psychics may build a safer base for consideration than blindly following the suggestions of only one. Any spiritually oriented psychic will not be offended by having you check within, for they know of what I speak. There are related thoughts to consider about the allied aspects of prophecy in the chapter on worship.

I said earlier that the speed of your brain operation has been increased through a higher consciousness vibration. We have introduced the idea that you are flowing into those true reality realms where one day your limitation of time will vanish into "the peace that passeth all understanding." Claim this identity as a cosmic being once more and use our thoughts and energy to assist your advancement, if you choose. We angels are your cousins in God's creation, and you need not be separated from us in consciousness unless you ignore that relationship.

You are now choosing the level of spiritual attainment you wish to demonstrate on earth. For those unwilling to choose peace, there will be a sorting out time. This time is not an eternal separation of energies, but merely a result of different reality choices and experiences. Label this choosing time what you will; nonetheless, *you are called to peace*. Then devote that remaining 80% of your time to living peacefully, and you cannot go astray.

Our energies surround you. Rise to us but ground your body simultaneously. It is earth's greatest challenge, humanity's finest opportunity. We invite your soul-sponsored, heartfelt participation.

Now, are there questions you would ask?

V.   You were discussing the ways in which human beings could learn to deal with these incoming energies without becoming stressed. Could you say more about meditation and other positive steps we might take?

U.   Meditation allows or encourages the individual to remove himself from an awareness of the physical life. Presently, we ask you to become more aware of the physical planet itself as a part of your meditation. Tune into the strength of the planet. Become aware of the trees so that you feel a part of the soil and roots. In other words, become more grounded in your meditation practices. Do not merely seek to go upward and out into space to escape the planet, but seek to go into the ground, also. Feel the planet's strength, feel its stability, feel its ability to take care of you. Renew and maintain your connectedness to the earth center. The reason for tuning into the spiritual or higher realms now is so that you will have greater soul consciousness. Bring that into alignment for service and caring for all life

141

on this planet. We have encouraged you to seek God. Do so but then bring that cosmic awareness back and connect it to the planet.

V.   How do you suggest that those of us who are already very busy do all these great peace ideas we have with 20% less time?

U.   Planning becomes essential. This planning would occur at the beginning of your day's activities, or at the end of your day for the next day's activities. Even both. Planning becomes absolutely essential in your usage of time. Taking time to plan allows you to accomplish more through superior functioning.

In a way we are talking about two methods of planning and how to balance them. Some humans will do better with the spiritual perception of looking back to the earth, looking back at themselves and their activities, and from that higher vantage point see what is not necessary and what adjustments need to be made. But for many people, tuning into the planet itself and working with it for most of their activities may be a more successful approach in this changing time. Use whichever method seems best. Understanding your existence is the vital thing. Although technology has developed considerable complexity, life has a very simple context. That context is valuing life. Where do you place your intentions, your feelings, your love, your caring? . . . your joy, your happiness, your sadness, all of your emotional parts? The purpose of this time acceleration is for you to value your life, your very existence. And then use it to gain peace through personal involvement in the events that affect you at the soul and body level. You must become a participant in protecting the planet itself and the family of life on this globe in space.

V.   How do individual and group meditations differ?

U.   Group meditation intensifies the energies attached to your intention for peace and preservation of all life. It assists with energizing a force field of thought, which is the tension on any given point or area. It does not effect time per se.

V.   Are you saying that a whole group of people meditating together have a higher consciousness than one person meditating?

U.   I'm saying that their togetherness amplifies the intensity of the electrical energies within an area, whether it be a room or a geographical area. The force field they generate is multiplied by the intensity of their thought. Meditation has to do with highly charging or amplifying the electrical charge of a thought, a place, an idea or a theme. Meditation doesn't affect time but it may give you a powerful experience of removing yourself from time. In meditation, or any concentrated and positive experience, you leave time's definitions and find reality.

V.   Could you say more about that?

U.   We angelic beings are not aware of density of form, so I cannot give you an explanation based on personal experience. To give you an idea of no-time (or universal awareness), I will use an example of what you call space beings and their experience with your time measurement. Imagine yourself in a spacecraft two million earth miles west of Jupiter. As you approach Jupiter you place your spacecraft on a grid line that will take you northwest of Jupiter on a course toward earth. As you move rapidly into earth's proximity, you look at a certain instrument on your control board. It indicates that a measurement process called time is used on planet earth. The closer you get, the more this instrument tunes into what the time measurement on that planet currently is. You make an adjustment with your equipment which then gives you access to earth's measurement plan.

As you go through a curtain or vapor of darkness, you simultaneously see light on the other side of the planet, so you are aware of the division of light and dark that relates to the time sequence of day and night. On your approach to the planet you observe that this time measurement changes on the planet, depending on where you are located. So you perceive there is a measurement used by this small planet that does not exist further out in the solar system, star system, or anywhere beyond the earth itself.

V.   So you're saying we are the only planet in our solar system that has time?

U.   There is one other place that has time, but it is not like yours. You are down to seconds and minutes, hours, days, weeks, months, years. Your entire existence is in increments of time that limit your return to higher consciousness. You box yourselves in with it.

For example, if you were driving your automobile at 10:00 P.M. on the 15th day of a month, and you are still in that automobile driving along at 1:00 A.M. the next morning on the 16th, you are still within the event. It is not over. Then why do you say it is past? According to your time measurement the 15th is gone, yet the event is still occurring. Whether you call it the 15th or the 16th, the event itself is the reality. Where is the logic of your time measurement?

It is not that I judge you personally, but our work for peace is made very difficult by your insistence on a linear measurement system when, in fact, space is not linear. Space curves. So we need to bring you back to consciousness of life as a series of events or experiences and upgrade your knowledge to the non-linear concept called hyperspace.

A part of my task in coming to you, then, is to change rigid perceptions that are invalid. Therefore, a large number of earth inhabitants will have to go through stages of consciousness education. This education will bring freedom to two groups ... you who presently live in the 3rd dimension, and also the souls presently out-of-body in the lower 4th dimension who have emotional attachment and power connection to the 3rd dimensional world you call earth living. I am repeating this for emphasis!

Some humans who live on earth are cleansing and freeing themselves of their 3rd dimensional limitations, their lower 4th dimensional thought rigidities, and are already operating with potential for the higher 4th or lower 5th dimensional reality. A very few have actually attained lower 5th consciousness already. However, at this moment in humanity's evolution, *your spiritual attainment of lower 5th dimensional reality can only be reached by practical actions to heal the planet.* No one can proceed into higher consciousness without participating for peace on earth and preservation of all life. I repeat. Only those who now aid the planet can achieve a high 4th dimensional state of conscious reality or possibly even a 5th.

You of earth have a challenge with great rewards ahead. May the Creator who has made our existence possible give you fortitude and courage to meet all challenges and reap many joys and rewards. We stand by you and with you in the unfolding of an incredible plan to rehabilitate this wondrous planetary creation through restitution of human responsibility.

V.   What's happening to plant growth patterns on the planet because of the increased vibratory change we are experiencing?

U.   We observe that some variance or increase is occurring. Your planet cycles of reproduction, seasonal changes, and growth are being affected with this increased vitality. Most areas only have faster growth or seasonal variation of a few minutes or hours, but in some cases seasons are ahead by weeks. Your equator, which is the half-way point between the north and south poles, has the most noticeable increase or change within growth cycles. It is in the area between 20 degrees north and 20 degrees south of this equator line that we observe the most obvious effects. The line located 20 degrees *north* of the equator has the most noticeable growth pattern changes, since this is one of the main avenues of energy contact or entry into the planet's atmosphere. In that location the surface of the planet itself is receiving a higher concentration of energy.

V.   May I ask whether that concentration affects stability of land masses?

U.   It has no effect. Earth is merely receiving a vitality caused by the amplification of more light. "More" meaning increased quantity with a higher vitality. Its vitality is just a slight degree of two or three percent higher than other places, yet that concentrated percentage does supply noticeably increased growth.

Since you still have "time," let me conclude my thoughts this way.

Once upon a time there was a beautiful planet called earth where peace, love and joy brought life's fulfillment to all inhabitants until the people fell under a dark cloud of negativity and dropped into a deep sleep filled with terrifying dreams of hate and war.

Because birds frequently flew over the planet and landed to bring many songs of that former joy and peace, a few people were awakening and prodding their friends to cease

146

the nightmare and remember how it had been long, long ago. Still the majority slept the dream of death.

Then a great white dove with glowing silver and gold radiance descended toward them sprinkling their minds and hearts with those powerful and sparkling rays of light. Gradually the inhabitants yawned, stretched and opened their eyes to see this glorious radiance. With their opening sight the great darkness vanished. Joy and peace were restored. Love's light embraced them once again.

In this tale, my cousins, there should be a happy ending, shouldn't there? But we need your cooperation to make it so. Will you receive the radiance? Will you open your eyes to God's truth?

A clarion call for peaceful action is now sounding to all potential doves on earth. Awaken, then, for earth is to be transformed. The nightmare must end.

Will you join with us to create a bright new existence of love and joy on earth?

147

Chapter VII

Peace

YOU DO NOT NEED WARFARE! Let no person, organization, or government persuade you otherwise. Your economy
does not need warfare to prosper. This very day there are new
ideas being developed even as in the past your radios, television, automobiles, and so on, were invented. A hundred years
ago you did not have your flying machines. *Think, think!* Let
your imagination free to soar among the clouds or the stars!
Peace time can be abundant if you wish it to be. Weapons are
destructive to life and planetary existence. Give them up.

We angels bring a spiritual impulse over the land to assist
in your awakening. As it blossoms be creative in peaceful
intention and actual products of living. Other planets and
lifeforms use inventions for peace, not war. You are called to
do the same.

The attitude that humanity generally holds about peace, as
it is currently expressed in the local and international cultures
of your planet, is not acceptable. What needs to be done to
bring a change in attitude and action by individuals and
groups will be the major focus of the information in this
chapter.

Let us begin with our definition of peace. Peace is the
harmonious interrelationship of all life, regardless of its form,
in a cooperative existence. A condition of peace allows each

form its individualized expression yet brings unity to an entire creation. Now this definition has not been fully practiced on your planet, and this fact needs to be acknowledged and immediately changed.

As time does not exist in our realm, but intention and events do, our intention becomes *immediate* in its expression. Consequently our present event or activity is to awaken you right now and support your practical actions to accomplish inner peace and peace as an externalized way of living. As an individualized soul energy you have both a full understanding of the peace ideal and an inner yearning for its completion. This desire for peace is built-in, so to speak, and is inherent in your soul's essence. Even a physical body yearns to live. Then live by achieving the goal of peaceful existence.

Because humanity's efforts toward peace have not succeeded, we will be recommending steps for the immediate future. Each soul is needed for healing the planet's difficulties and has been called forth by Lord Jesus, the Great Rays, and now myself.

This Time of Awakening is to *awaken* that inner memory, that peace quality, so that you will bring harmlessness to life on your planet. We applaud whatever means you use to demonstrate and express this inherent quality of harmony and cooperation.

On your planet there are individuals and organizations that have the seed or spark of this inherent unity burning brightly within. We therefore totally support such individuals and organizations for their *intention*. Because intention is only the beginning and not the final result, great concentrated effort and action must now follow. You have many helpful organizations, but we perceive they are going outward in different directions without a common connection or unified focus.

Like a wheel with many spokes, the spokes must retain the central and unified concept in all that is done for peace, for life's preservation. Then realign some energy of those outward spokes back to the central point from which they generate their being. It is time to practice intermingling all organizations toward the one common cause humanity must achieve. We need your broad coherence, whatever your organizational basis. We need your combined intention, your energized presentation of self and group for the one purpose.

This time is not a moment for separation but for energized group intention. It is the instant to see purity within each individual, certainly, yet the greatest calling is for unity at organizational levels, as well. This unity has many benefits. Your electro-magnetic power reaches its maximum potential when you unite with others.

Now let us clarify those words *energy* and *consciousness* that are so frequently used these days on earth. Energy is vitality or power, the "electrical current" that supplies your existence. It is God's cosmic essence; it is the source of life. Consciousness is awareness and intelligence. It can be your individualized consciousness, the consciousness of the planet or the consciousness of the universe. It has many aspects and various levels, whether from thoughts or actions.

The most supreme level of Universal Mind has the sum total (like a library) of all that exists and has existed through the thought process. You can use this immense knowledge for ideas and practical applications. You are encouraged to use the intelligence of your awakening group and organizational alliances to achieve group-powered consciousness. You truly can see beyond the limiting negative information stored around your planet and not be detoured in your spiritual awakening as members of an empowered movement for peace.

Our recommendations to quickly move you into peace are these. Use your quiet times to tune into the dimensions of existence beyond your physical awareness. As you tune into this greater consciousness you will be able to utilize cosmic intelligence to expand your thinking and perception. Second, if you have already healed and cleansed your own personal natures and committed your dedication to the planet and all lifeforms, now take this commitment to the group level and amalgamate the separate energies into one rich core of expression.

Throughout this document the key phrase *responsibility for individuals* has become evident. Now encourage groups and organizations to implement this *common responsibility* to model an even greater human potential through group consciousness and its extraordinary creative power.

This present cycle of our spiritual impulse energies feeds and fuels *group participation*, and the intertwining of many groups for an intense power base of action for peace. Yes, do that which you call networking. Meet one another, express your individuality. But go forward from there to weave a peace tapestry in which all of you have the same pattern in mind. By focusing that commitment into one design, the planet will greatly benefit.

You are one family. One planet. There is currently one God-design to unfold on earth and that is peace.

Your personal and group involvement is immediately required to reclaim awareness of that design and accept participation in it. As you move toward the acceptance of who you are and why you are here, let the synchronization of many soul memories come together with intense creative purpose. Move toward the joy that is available in that mutual endeavor.

As I am a powerful dove to excite and ignite your activity for our one cause, so also are you doves needed to flock to the completion of our task. In this second coming of higher consciousness, your model groups of peace are few but growing and shall light a long-darkened path of planetary forgetfulness and habitual negativity.

From that spark of spiritual impulse, a bright inner spark of knowing within each person will now feel a stirring. For some it will be only a flicker, for others an evident movement. For some it will be such a shift that their lives will change quickly, even radically. It will be evident to many via soul awareness that they cannot continue to be part of group thought that moves the planet toward destruction.

Peace is flying among you on the wings of a mighty dove and will soon land. It is not creeping in like a soft fog or a morning mist. It is winging down among you, seeking a place to light and call forth true intention for peace that is soul-resident within you.

Many of you speak about peace, yet there is no place within your thoughts and activities for it to mature. Words without substance behind them are hollow. Would you seek a decaying hollow tree to make a bridge over a stream? Or would you seek a more substantial one to hold your weight? Likewise, many persons and organizations state that they are for peace, yet most demonstrate no substantive action though called to do so. Their inactivity is a great loss to all life.

This descending, inspiring spiritual impulse we bring is for growth and action. Then take action against the concept of oppression, person to person, nation to nation to make changes. No matter the technological trappings, no matter the differences in clothing, food, housing or environment, you are all human. Your basic quality is that of a soul living within a human body. Somehow it seems that you are ashamed to be human. Is it because humans have done so many cruel and heartless things? Remove all the exterior trappings, whether they be man-made or environmental, and in your nakedness you see the sameness to all other humans. In your body functions and emotions most desires and needs are the same worldwide, are they not? Millions of you cry in loneliness even as you constantly move away from each other. Acknowledge the sameness! Move your energies together. *See* and *feel* your unity with each other. Why are some depriving others of food, water, clothing, shelter, improved environment, happiness and joy? Why do some refuse to share their abundance? The joys of life belong to everyone. *Each person has a right to joy, love and peace. These are absolute human rights that you are surrendering.* Absolute and necessary human rights! Retain them; they are God-granted. Then allow the full purity of humanity's soul nature to purge the negative and express only the brighter life, for you are the most unique design ever put into the created form of matter.

You are encouraged to have peaceful *group* consciousness and effective group activity to solve present problems. Be creative in working together without intent to dominate. Learn the skills of close cooperation. It is a challenging, stimulating, satisfying process. It is the experience before you that must be learned.

I am here to bring you together. Each of you can fly separately, yet you belong in the safety and unity of the total flock. You are an individualized soul expanding through love and service. You are a soul now encouraged to care for the planet and the welfare of all humanity. Naturally in caring for humanity you care for yourself.

Within this Time of the Dove a great cleansing will take place for many humans as the conflicts of soul and outer personality increase and become evident. As an individual you will increase your inner awareness; you *will change*. It can be a forward or backward change, however.

The soul may have to struggle to establish or maintain its dominion over distracting personality desires that must be released. The empowered spiritual impulse I bring will shake many humans up, to a greater or lesser degree. Still others will be soothed, comforted and greatly inspired into purposeful action. All depends on attitude and willingness. By our contact, humanity's need for unity will be strengthened. Your past minutes of prayer and hour-long meditation for peace have been helpful but not consistent. It is necessary for the masses to think and act peacefully in a daily, dependable fashion. There is no other way out of your dilemma. Now, pause here in your reading and contemplate this next question.

Is there any reason why *you* cannot be peaceful? Think a while on this before you give your answer, please.

★ ★ ★ ★ ★ ★ ★ ★ ★ ★ ★ ★ ★

If there is a reason for your lack of peace, commit to resolve that reason or problem and move boldly into a new world of clear perception and service.

The inner consciousness that emanates from your soul is creative, harmonious, joyful, wise, reverent and peaceful. When the body's intelligence accepts the soul's desire and plan for peace, it becomes a living Christ-in-the-flesh or a spiritual energy in human form. This evolutionary design of love expressing in matter is your salvation or enlightened status made manifest. Because we see only a few of you living this inner unspeakable joy, we come to empower a rapid opening for change to that greater level of consciousness.

The inner consciousness sees everything from a center point of love and nurturing. It sees love in everything. Therefore, during this Time of Awakening the inner self will be strengthened by our teaching, and the runaway aspects of human personality will be brought into balance and alignment. This will be an opportunity to realize that an unwilling personality can neither reach high consciousness nor express peace. It is hoped that this uncooperative personality will eventually surrender to the soul and say, "My way of fighting doesn't work. It's exhausting. Help me!!"

The Silver Ray has told you climatic changes will occur. They are happening now. You are a soul in a physical body, and when the human being is cold, thirsty or hungry it becomes aware of the physical condition. We do not wish you to suffer, yet these climatic changes are part of the consciousness raising that will *probably* happen. Sometimes you must encounter difficulty before you to turn to each other and discover the "goodness" there. You need each other! Spiritually you all know each other, even if you do not recognize it at the physical level yet.

Our Harmonic Convergence energy in August, 1987, made you collectively more aware of the planet and its physical needs whatever other ideas you have about its purpose. Your planet is a GREEN planet. All that introduces life and sustains it is green or relates to this growth-granting color. Look at the trees, the plants, the grass and things that sprout from the soil itself. All of these things relate to green. The olive branch in your biblical story of Noah and the flood was a green branch. The vitality of your planet relates to the color green. As you become more peaceful within yourself you will relate to the physical planet more closely.

As the waters of the oceans are affected by the gravitational pull and the earth's waters feel the force of the moon, you also feel the effect of the moon and the Silver Ray on you. This will come through to you as a nurturing aspect, as a definite caring for the physical planet.

During this influence of The Dove you will personally and collectively begin to design ways to have peace now. You will explore ways to make peace applicable. The darkness of destruction is a great cloud over the thinking of humanity. It is likened to a thick fog that prevents the sunlight from penetrating.

I will swoop to stir that fog so the sun and moon's ray will strike the earth with spiritual impulse, bounce back upwards and dissipate the fog. As each of you is being called individually, you will feel the need for your personal participation in everyday activities for lasting peace.

You exist! Now, what will you do with that existence? This question is the most important one you will ever be asked, or ever have to answer, as an individual soul.

This document is entitled Descent of the Dove because The Dove of Peace is landing on the earth. Empowered with a sparkling rainbow radiance, I bring stirring changes to the planet. My gratitude is extended to the eagle people on the blue Ray of Intention who have opened the way for my energy. The time of these intelligent ones has been very intense and active. They have gathered, and will gather, many souls ready to harken to the strength and power of the eagle with its great outstretched wings and wondrous vision. Yet the eagle will soon fly to its mountaintop ledge and guard the arrival of The Dove. Ever watchful and wise it gathered those who waited and will now protect the multiple flocks needed to fulfill heaven's purpose.

Doves and rainbows (like eagles) are meaningful symbols. Have you ever wondered why you chose the rainbow as your symbol for the New Age? It is a reminder of your own connection with the creative energies of the universe ... with God and the Great Rays of gold and silver. You see, your soul knows about your inner Ray of Intention and its supplemental rays. It knows about the importance and vitality of color. Color, color! You and your world are color! And you thrill to the rainbow color bath Silver Ray has placed around the entire globe.

The soul also knows about doves, your symbol of peace. Because the soul knows harmony, it wants to live and demonstrate that knowledge while in its physical body. The soul would like to stay and enjoy the full potential of that body container and this special evolutionary occasion.

Yes, your soul knows that the dove has been designated the symbol of true peace on your planet. Its qualities of love and gentle strength are the factors that will bring peace and make it last. What words do each of you say and want to hear?

I LOVE YOU.

Is not the dove also the symbol of love? and peace?

Your soul knows these things and has been endeavoring to express them for years (earth time). Now during this Time of Awakening it is all coming together through soul expression and further cosmic revelation.

Now is the time of the doves. It is the period designated for dove-like (gentle-hearted) people to gather together and sing a new song of peace. It is an event intended for sharing the harmonic unity of love. Come forward, then, and feel the abiding presence of the all-encompassing Creator as God's energy, through The Rays, seeks to embrace you in the sky-bright rainbow envelope of peace.

158

You are *in* Universal Mind. You are part *of* Universal Mind. Therefore, you are love. Whatever circumstances may evolve, whether happy or tragic by your standards, each individual will eventually reach out to another person and want to give and receive LOVE. It is inherent in each of you. It is also inherent in you to be free of the uncommitted, unwilling personality, though this may require effort. During this Time of the Dove you will be led to unity in all factors of existence.

An abiding melody of color and sound echoes through the soul of each person. For some it is a haunting, lingering refrain experienced as the clarity of purpose. For others it is almost totally forgotten in the deafening noise of earth life. Nonetheless, there is an ancient melody of peace retained within the recesses of your God-mind and soul experience.

As you learn to be still and go into that beautiful place of your *true self* you will hear that melody. It is the sound of the universe, the celestial pulse that vibrates for you and all life. Your consciousness moves on it, within it, and is energized by it. It is the rhythm of life where no personality judgment exists, where harmony alone vibrates in its rich, healing quality. *This cosmic hymn, humans of earth, is peace.*

Most of you have experienced this in depth only a few times in your life, if at all, yet in the vibratory resonance we now bring it will increase, increase and increase to transform your mind to heavenly constancy. Yet, as a lifeform with that experimental quality called free will, you must desire it. *You must choose it.*

It will become more evident as the immediate months and their activities unfold that each person must absolutely, without any hesitation or evasion, speak the truth of personal belief to others and begin to participate in peace endeavors. Several things are probable occurrences within the next 14 to 18 months especially.

The world itself is going to become separated and segregated by political activities within certain nations and by activities of the reigning political leaders in each country. Some countries and leaders may remain silent in the beginning of our energy changes, yet by the end of the 14 to 18 months they will have to indicate their status. No nation can remain a non-participant in the issues that concern the planet.

These issues will be multi-leveled. There will be the issues of spiritual freedom and freedom of worship. There will be the issue of political peace. Pollution issues of the environment must be solved. Social issues of poverty, health, shelter, education, and the more humane aspects of life will have to be addressed by each nation, and by that of your global government.

The interrelationship of each individual, group and nation, will become more evident as you use political governance to end war and solve environmental concerns. The political arena must truly become concerned about the environment and preservation of life. *Politics is the opportunity to achieve harmonious solution to human problems.* It is the avenue for creative soul input to earth living conditions. Those who call themselves spiritual may say they have no responsibility in that arena because it is "too dirty." Who better to change that negative quality than the soulful? Let government become the soul's purview and see what can happen. Souls have no *special* interests, only the desire for equitable human rights everywhere. When the political arena becomes a harmonious intention for good, your world will change very rapidly.

I wish to elaborate on this further, but first I ask for your questions.

V.   How does the individual participate in all of this?

U.   It will become more evident as the rapid and impacting changes occur in the next 14 to 18 months that

Peace

each individual must speak out for the environment and safety of the physical planet. Those who become involved in organizational and pressure groups will combine energies for more rapid influence. Churches must act for *human rights*, too. You cannot divide the spiritual from its practical application of love. Choose an activity that you feel strongly about and move from words to actual demonstration of your belief in these issues. You will not be able to say, "*Someone must do something.*" It will come into your awareness that *you* need to speak and act for yourself. Each individual must participate, must move forward with these things, for you are an individual soul with individual responsibilities.

Whatever your recognition of the problem, please communicate this and act in support of humane activities. As stated, you have an inner knowing if you only listen within. The reverence for God, the reverence for life and the personal expression of peace on earth have been the hallmarks of all great humans. Now join together in political clarity and spiritual persistence for positive change wherever your soul points.

Since all is connected, you can move from your concern for the planet itself to an understanding of the need for stopping hydrogen and nuclear destructiveness. Or, if you wish to begin with stopping war and its destructiveness and then work backwards to clean-up the planet, do so.

All of this activity relates to the one human need: peace and preservation of life. Yes, by all means, stop the destructiveness! There are others on the planet working with that same concern. But some may help by cleaning up your air, water and land. This same intention for peace, however it expresses, is valuable and all are needed.

V.   You said that we really need 1/3 of the whole human population actually involved in peace measures, so

161

there is a major criticalness in all of this. If we attend to the things that immediately threaten us would that secure more time to solve the environmental problems?

U.   Yes, stop using destructive devices. Wars must end! Yet a realignment of environmental issues for the continuance of life is essential, also. Both are needed!

V.   A common question is asked regarding national defense. How can we give up weapons when evil exists and those of negative intent are constantly warring on the peaceful?

U.   There is a collective consciousness on your globe that seeks to justify combat with an attack-and-defend attitude. Yet within the intelligence of God there is no justification for the deliberate killing of another human, including self. Just as you have developed rituals of worship, so have you advanced your rituals of warfare for physical, emotional and spiritual domination of others. The spiritual part *always* seeks to escape because the soul knows that imprisonment, destruction, and lack of reverence are against its inherent nature.

Therefore, defense is as illogical as attack. The occurrence of a disaster, man-made or "natural," proves this point, for when another is injured or needs assistance, differences dissolve, and any personal barriers are usually forgotten. When a person or nation cries out for help, the soul's desire to assist normally overrides the personality's sense of selfishness and territory.

V.   Is any spiritual censoring, or karma, created beyond this lifetime by choosing a military career for personal livelihood?

U.   Presently on your planet, you believe that war and its subsequent murder can be separated into two aspects: attack and defense. I shall comment accordingly. Those

162

nations and their military personnel who engage in provoked attack, or war, on another nation or group of people are under karmic circumstances. All of the attacking personnel who cause harm are responsible for the land area and for *each* human and ensouled animal form destroyed. Any deliberate attack that overrides another's free will and causes mortal harm is karmic and must be balanced at a later time.

Understand that only for a short period will karmic release be granted for the defenders of any nation that deliberately prepares the machinery of war even as a defensive mode. Why? Because they are preparing to attack, or retaliate, with murder, also, even though they may not have been the originators of the initial thrust.

Your planet's consciousness has such a stench of war and evil that this basic attitude and its conditions must be changed. Again, you may wonder why. My reply is simple. When you prepare for destructiveness, you set the brain thought pattern on murder. The thought of murder is absolutely unacceptable to soul integrity. What your human war thought does is override soul integrity and fill the intelligence with a bombardment of murderous intent.

Murder is not allowable. War is murder.

I have come to change the negative human thought patterns so prevalent here and so totally unacceptable by any definition of divine order or galactic civilization.

The brain and its memory storage process has been influenced, propagandized and trained to believe killing is natural. For the soul, a lover of peace, this is a lie, and it cries "Stop! Stop!" This dichotomy creates an imbalance between soul knowing and body intelligence. Any information about attack and defend that is received and filed may cause a major distortion in the perception of an individual, group or nation.

Killing is not approved because it changes a being's soul expression and opportunity for growth and service.

Any negative data received in military training from the planet's destructive thought form, or encultured teaching that tells the brain storage unit to kill or destroy is evil, indeed. Creating a basic untruth like this about the one universal law of life, which the soul well knows, can create untold agony in a human life.

Murder and war and violence are an antithetical concept to the soul, and it considers all such negative information *false*. This fact is why most soldiers feel, at the least, distaste and remorse even as they kill. Mental illness is a common response to the battlefield experience. The soldiers are humans; they were not born to kill. All souls are born to respect life.

As stated, only for a limited time will we allow those nations who defend themselves from unprovoked attack to remain free from any karmic burden and consequences. This means, on earth, that you may block attack only at the moment of its thrust. There must be no prior intention to destroy the attacking lifeforms!

In previous lifetimes most karmic consequences of your human war and destructive actions have not been directly experienced while on earth. You have died and then been taught in another dimension. Your soul review, as military soldiers, took place either immediately upon death, or in a later, more structured evaluation. Always there have been out-of-body consequences for each murderous event because God's universal ordinance still remains: DO NOT KILL!

Now, in the Time of the Dove, there is a probable spiritual program planned to give *immediate*, on-earth awareness to the danger and consequences of any and all warlike acts. It does not take a large event to set off a chain of great destructiveness using the "high tech" weapons you have created, so you must acquire positive global consciousness very quickly.

In our probable educational program we will highlight the causes of many highly destructive events that have already been set in motion by your earth groups and nations. Our realms will call these negative circumstances and events to your attention and utilize them to teach humanity both individually and collectively that you may not misuse God's energy.

To prepare for defense draws you into the same thought process and patterns used by the possible attackers. When you acquire the same thought pattern of attack and defense, you are in a same destructive mode even though you say the attackers are the evil ones and you are pure because you "did not throw the first stone." *The attitude of harmlessness is the basis of peace.* This was the teaching of both Buddha and Lord Jesus. What does it mean "to turn the other cheek?"

Humanity must now experience directly what it causes to finally learn that destructiveness is absolutely ungodly and will not be allowed on this planet any longer. Cause and effect is a universal law. Learn this eagerly and apply it immediately to release all concepts of murder, violence and war you may have received in your brain's storage area. Cleanse yourselves and be healed.

Those who engage in military careers as a life work are overriding their soul caring through false personality beliefs. The inherent yearning of the soul is to preserve life, not destroy it. The guilt and heavy burdens that start, grow and fester in the thoughts of those who kill are because they go against the soul's nature. How many war veterans are truly happy to have been killers, medals or not?

You are given medals and much prideful fanfare in an attempt to assuage your soul's pain and convince you that your action was noble. Take off the medals. Put down your guns. *Where are the medals for establishing and maintaining peace?*

All of your choices and actions are in the cause/effect cycle, and if a military career requires you to kill, that is a moral choice. Actions involving the taking of another's life could require balancing in current life experience and cause karmic effects.

Rather than continue with the attitude of national defense, it is better to think of *national and global preservation.* Begin to consider each individual as a spark of God's creation worthy of existence on this planet. You are all in this situation together. Some of you choose not to see the required unity in your world situations, yet all circumstances ultimately affect all peoples.

Earth is one elliptical homeland in space requiring harmony and the conscious dominion of peace. Achieve this by first releasing thoughts of violence and fear and then by joining together for life's divine purpose.

Now I shall pause and respond to your questions. Please take a moment's quietude before we continue, however.

V. Thank you, Uriel. What is political action and who should do it?

U. Many actions are political because politics is your process of group governance. But some actions are more obvious and direct. With the planet's nuclear war danger, for example, and your underground hydrogen explosions, neither citizens nor governments can ignore action.

Let me clarify this. The first level of governance is personal. In it is the absolute statement by each person, "I am for peace and I now demonstrate that belief with my actions."

Evolving from that belief can be demonstration of either
or both areas of concern already mentioned: Preservation of
all Life—Peace on Earth. Caring for the physical planet
allows life to continue at a higher level of purity and joy in
earth's environment. That is why the second level requires
that two or more gather and then expand their joint commitment into group expression. As creative group responsibility for life activities is assumed, a planetary citizenry
level is reached. All of these levels are a soul awareness
response that those in power cannot be allowed to take
away your inalienable human right to life.

Peace is not the abandonment of human action. It is a
spiritual/physical agreement and expression to sustain life
harmoniously. It is our angelic perception that Lord Jesus
recognized how greatly each individual needed peace
within and gave an example to be followed, knowing that
those seeds would bear fruit and bring our present cycle
great clarity and support. Jesus was involved in life!

The truly peaceful soul, heart and mind combination
helps others become responsible so that the many peaceful
ones can create what you call heaven on earth. You do not
need to die to find heaven. With the release of your
misbelief, you can achieve together a high spiritual consciousness on earth right now through creative beliefs and
behavior. Since the days of Lord Jesus and other great ones,
your planet has developed monstrous weaponry capable of
annihilating much of life and possibly the planet itself.
Then we now call all of you forward to prevent these things.

When many agree that peace is possible, heaven will
grow from a weak and helpless concept to a manifested
experience involving an entire planetary family. That is
why I, and so many others, are here to lend support. But
you are the solution to, as well as the cause of, earth's

167

problems. When you join your creative God-qualities with those of others like yourself, you become heaven, my cousins. You return to peace.

V.   What can we do with the situation where people say they want peace but do not become personally peaceful or attend to the planet's welfare, either one?

U.   Yes, this behavior is observed. We are seeking to have you change. In all things, the key is *unity*. The collective voice, composed of your individual powers is highly influential. If you take two of you, 10 of you, 100, 1,000, 10,000, 100,000, 1, 2 or 3 million and expand that to 3 billion at one time, preferably within a 28-day period, you can totally change earth's destiny. Smaller numbers are useful because they are catalysts for peace, lend reverence for life, and can offer a change of consciousness to positively affect other human thoughts. However, due to the free will factor used only on this planet, *higher consciousness vibrations do not ensure a change in each individual's behavior!* Reread that last sentence, please, for it is a limitation that we angels must incorporate in our rehabilitation program and process.

V.   You stated previously that it would take us 327,000 earth years to change our consciousness from negative to positive if we only meditated and did not act to clean up our problems.

U.   Yes, actual individual action for peace must occur. Therefore, whether you call it individual peace or political peace, by our definition, *political decisions begin where two or more are gathered*, not just in town halls and council chambers. Those official governments, however, have too long been involved with power and its leverage over others. Take these incoming vibrations to change power politics for the *politics of love*.

It has been noted and recommended that mass communication be used as your tool for moving the mountain of human
ignorance and inaction. Use your television, movies, your
printed words and publications, your radio and any personal
or technological means that can be used to unite people.
Speak, confer and inspire, as your patriots did, to establish
the patterns that ensure human rights. Then state the dangers
of your destructive devices and attitudes, along with solutions.
Be persuasive and persistent for human life. We need *planetary patriots* as never before. Hurry with your skills and
intelligence to reach the many who are ready to awaken. We
are stimulating your thought process with high vibration
precisely so you can listen within for soul guidance and
intuitive wisdom and follow through with useful activities.

We perceive that each individual is part of the political
"machinery" in any given area, whether in pairs, small or
large groups, or nations. Therefore, use the voice of your
belief and your intention for peace to participate in changing
local, national and international power politics to the politics
of love. This discussion has ignited my soul feeling to say
more about practical applications and movements that are
helping, or could help you establish peace, so let us omit
other questions.

On behalf of the angelic realms I wish to acknowledge
those many excellent efforts you have begun already for the
establishment of peace and preservation of all life. Some
ideas and applications have been gradually evolving while
others represent a more dramatic change in applied
awareness. All interests I will mention are valuable and
necessary and provide a way for every soul's Ray of Intention
to be useful in this life.

For some years you will notice the United States and
Western Europe have been moving toward understanding what

you term "psychology" (study of the soul) or at least study of the human personality. The wisest counselors and therapists have realized that the personality is a partner or tool of the soul and cannot be healed of its problems until this recognition is applied. Thus many books have appeared about loving attitudes and how to love unconditionally, allowing the development of transpersonal approaches to behavior. This holistic approach is a growing movement to cleanse a sleeping society of its violent attitudes and separation from true reality.

Growth in your metaphysically oriented churches and groups is especially noted along with the increasing practice of prayer, quiet times, meditation and contemplation, back-to-nature excursions, walks, even solo jogging activities.

What is termed holistic health care and its approach to life through eating living food for proper diet and nutrition, massage and structural body care, exercise and rest, herbs and natural healing agents, and various energy balancing modes is encouraging. As our time acceleration pattern may create the possibility of human stress, this holistic living attitude must continue and grow. Holy means whole.

"Return to the land" individuals and groups who are true caretakers of the planet are much needed, and a few are trickling back from the cities into rural areas. Those farmers and agriculturists who have been consistent in their use of non-toxic pesticides and development of safe land practices are acknowledged and encouraged to even greater practices. This feeling of loving the land was accelerated by the Harmonic Convergence of August 17, 1987, and remains within the planet's vibration even now.

Conservation of natural resources and ecological concerns are growing as truly they must. Your many peoples and nations have polluted the air, fresh and ocean waters, soils and continue to destroy the few remaining forests that are your

170

breathing bulwark for life. Further and immediate attention must be given to solar and alternative power sources, resolution of "acid rain" and ozone problems, neutralization of toxic wastes and the evil probability of atomic, nuclear and hydrogen mishaps (those not war initiated and intended).

Animal slaughter of all kinds is finally receiving some humane opposition, and an increasing awareness of the value of animals stirs in your hearts. You have seen that land and sea mammals are important. Whales and dolphins, otters and seals, as well as the declining land breeds, which you call "endangered," must be protected. You are their caretakers, too, as you must care for all the planet in every aspect. You were given dominion by God and the Great Rays. Use it wisely and creatively.

In what you call international trade you should continue to seek a balanced sharing back and forth. However, the huge cartels that support weaponry and war must end, and the small groups who now literally control all monetary systems of your world must be stopped. You seem to be totally unaware and powerless, even at governmental levels, to deal with this evil process. If you do not notice and take responsibility, a great financial Armageddon will occur.

One very positive move we note is the attempt of a few governments to seek peace with each other, brought about by true humanitarian principle, we hope, and not just fear of alien forces in space. But it is you, the people, in ever-growing dissatisfaction, who are feeling the need for inner and external peace. It is you we see creating organizations at the citizen level, you who walk and march for that issue, you who write letters, talk on the radio and affect TV and movies toward that higher noble goal.

We notice how even your entertainers are making their feelings known in positive song lyrics these days, which is

171

extremely important because you repeat them as mantras, so to speak. A true musical contribution to human thinking offers a message of love and peace, not the emotional lamentations we hear you incorporating into most of your popular songs.

All repetitive messages become part of your brain memory. Songs of immoral content and inanity are so frequent that you become programmed to moral weakness and decadence. You watch TV programs with a constant stream of drivel and uninspiring content. The very tool of instantaneous communication released to you for the creation of planetary peace has had quite the opposite affect, for the most part.

Yes, there are occasional uplifting programs of moral value, and great music, but they are few and far between. The planet's road to enlightenment is filled with the detours of human ignorance, laziness, noise and general unconsciousness. You must begin to use all areas of communication, such as TV, movies, radio, and all printed formats, to stress good news, to teach peace and to identify particular problems in need of correction. This step is critical. It does you no good to create schooling systems for the young to study important issues and then not find support in society for their peaceful ideals to unfold. *Education, communication, and inner awareness cannot be separated.* With such pervasive negativity around the world do you wonder why drug and alcohol problems persist and suicides increase?

I most especially want to acknowledge any political leader, ruler, politician or party, watch-dog organization or citizen who works to stop violence and war's expression from inflaming the globe. Only from your efforts do we see growth, for you are the God-expression given dominion or responsibility for your 3rd dimensional planet's course.

The underground hydrogen explosions, though never openly communicated about by your major powers, is absolutely the most critical issue you face. We cannot save you from ripping the tectonic plates of the planet apart, or prevent you from exploding atomic and nuclear war devices at each other. The new horror weapons have such potential impact on life that you should be shouting "stop" from every mouth. We angels cannot do the work for you, but our aid and dedication are available to help you do the work that awaits. Only you in your soul wisdom, moral integrity and physical actions can change that pattern because you *are peace*. Do you remember? YOU ARE PEACE!

Yes, peace lies within you and must now be firmly rooted in your mind and heart as a gift to self and all of life, including this immense and exquisite garden spot you volunteered to attend. Gardening is a full-time job. Life must be watched and assisted constantly. There are no abandonments permitted.

I remind you that life truly began in that unimaginable time when The One who caused it all gave birth to a sacred excursion of creative, spiritual/physical masterpieces. A portion of that vast masterpiece included formation of *hyperspace* or a curving womb now impregnated with what is called existence. And you are a small part of that life excursion. There is so much of it that only God and its first two offspring can see it all. Still we all belong to that mystery and expressive glory, and our soul's beauty is a passport throughout the universal diadems of peace. On your small suffering planet earth, you die to defend the peace by practicing war. Therefore we come to help you defend human rights peacefully and live to enjoy those fruits.

Even as we angels have our own realms, you have physical life cousins on Saturn and Jupiter, and also those who reside in areas of the Pleiades, Orion and Sirius. So expand your thinking to truly understand that space curves, and one day soon you may meet other physical lifeforms through visitations across hyperspace. Hyperspace is there waiting for you to understand just as electricity was always there waiting for you to "discover" it. In this lifetime you and your space family may yet meet to exchange information and ideas.

The Pleiades inhabitants are a primary example of how physical life energies get along intelligently and harmoniously. In fact, the primary characteristics of the Pleiadians are balance, law, order and harmony . . . the latter being the most important. The former three interrelate with the last one forming a platform for peaceful existence. What you call a negative ray once tried to influence the Pleiadians approximately 200,000 years ago (your time) to no avail. When there is harmony, that peacefulness provides an unshakable foundation. This may be within an individual, family group, nation, or planet.

Other star groups that may have once experienced warlike thoughts have chosen to formulate and maintain the principle that WARFARE IS NOT ALLOWED! Consequently, any lifeform energy persisting with warlike or murderous thoughts is isolated for an unlimited time during which an evaluation process is completed. In the Pleiadian star cluster an exchange of information is made from the unpeaceful individual to a selected committee that in turn gives input back to the individual so that accurate communication and idea exchange occurs. Both sides present their views, a discussion evolves, and a decision agreeable to both groups is made. If an issue is not fully resolved, a time period is determined for experimenting with ideas from all parties concerned to achieve a workable plan. Then the lifeform makes its final decision to be peaceful or not. If the ruling committee decides that the individual lifeform truly does not wish to be peaceful, it is exiled to a region where the Rebel Ray is in charge. Thus it can continue its existence as it chooses without gross destruction to other peaceful life and matter areas. This exile is accomplished by using the coordinates of the Rebel Ray's location, and the lifeform is delivered there by a Pleiadian spacecraft.

Earth cannot follow this procedure until her planetary conduct in the solar system is determined to be peaceful. There is, at present, no peace reliably demonstrated from your population, so you are not allowed to utilize banishment and other solutions until that changes. (Incidentally, earth has never been used as a dumping ground for exiling evil ones from other stars or planets, lest your mind is contemplating such a thought.) Now that I have mentioned other lifeforms in space, how do you feel? Are you beginning to get ready for that trip among the stars after your planet is healed and humanity is stable?

Your star travel must be a peaceful journey with harmonious intent! Moreover, you may become host to a peaceful visit from other lifeforms first, since you cannot yet make the journey to them, and they already have the knowledge available for visiting you, as some do now. Understand that the Great Rays have intervened on this planet and are using spiritual and angelic support rather than technological, wherever possible. We shall see how far our influence and inspiration reach for urgent change. Are you psychologically and emotionally ready for such an adventure? There are many surprising wonders ahead for those who unfetter their limitations, fill their hearts with love and implement their soul's intention.

I, Uriel, The Dove and your Archangel of Peace, am here to lead and to guide you from your current hatreds, wars and

175

storms of discontent and confusion. Within your measurement of time this is a major historical occasion. I recommend you become soul-receptive each day. During these days of exploration and growth, be sure to be still, feel the warmth of the sunshine whenever you can. Then, in the star-studded sky, glance at the moon, and let its beams softly illuminate your way so that the night is ever bright. As you look at the stars and wander by thought into their exquisite patterns, know that some of your family is out there among those living places where the wisdom of The Dove is known.

Somewhere in the dimensions of higher consciousness we angels hope to meet and celebrate your victorious accomplishment for peace here on earth. Until we can congratulate you in that finer accomplishment, I send this prayer onward, my cousins, to strengthen and support you in our mutual task for peace.

> Oh, Almighty-Source-of-Life, pour your pure essence upon this planet ever brighter. Let your radiance be seen and known in that experience called time, as well as in the great beyond. Let peace settle into earth's hologram and express outward from every soul, heart, mind and action throughout your magnificent expansion of life never-ending.

> Answer me and answer all humans who acknowledge you. Give forth continual energy for personal and global peace on this especially beautiful planet creation.

> We thank you for the abundance that you have given, are giving and will continue to give.

In reverence,

Uriel

Chapter VIII

Clarion Call

Across the distances of space millions of spiritual energies are rushing to assist you. Hurry! is the watchword. An emergency DANGER signal emits its siren from the surface of your planet to angelic realms. What has gone wrong? Can the technological madness that has taken hold for war be stopped? be healed?

Thousands of "wise ones" on the planet are telling you and other listeners that your personality or ego is causing difficulties and preventing a heavenly environment. Activities of many kinds related to caring and nurturing humans and conserving a diseased planet are surfacing. Millions of copies of books and other print and non-print sources are being sold as guidelines for you to follow. Read the books, go to your group meetings, look at your visual-information screens, but above all tear off the blinders of ignorance and disinterest. As you pull back the veil from over your eyes, let the light of truth dazzle you into clear perception and vital awareness.

You already know the answers to all important questions. You already *know* what to do. There is that inner voice within that leads you to completion of soul purpose. You are in God's radiance; do you remember? You are in the rainbow radiance; do you sense it? The rainbow is around your earth to heal you, to reveal current developments and align your soul with our spiritual endeavor and support.

Are you ready to create peace? Can you handle the challenge? I think you can! The great Silver Ray thinks you can. The powerful Gold Ray thinks you can! Your relatives from the Pleiades, Orion and Sirius think you can! And comrades from your own solar system are also lending guidance and assistance. So this very instant let us unite and *change* your world. Praise be sung to the Originator-of-all-life which is constant in its caring and in its wish for us to continue life.

Due to your 5 billion inhabitants, most of whom are working from the personality and not the soul level, the thought forms in the consciousness of the planet are quite negative. We seek rapid change, rapid action for peace at the global level. There is a need for an impact of planetary thought and influence to immediately motivate peaceful action. To be able to do this quickly and sustain the impetus, I have indicated the ideal number of 3 billion is needed to put you permanently out of the danger zone.

The forcefulness of this large a number of persons will be like an electrical battery charged to its full amplification, allowing all to use it for higher awareness.

We recognize that a number such as 1, 2, or 3 billion people is immense, and I certainly have no wish to overwhelm you. Yet we urge you to work toward a goal of 3 billion awakened souls just as soon as possible, because we really need 67% of humanity learning to focus upon peace. So many humans are half-hearted, inconsistent, and only partially willing to acquire inner personal peace. Thus do we struggle toward a universal spiritual level where a stable opportunity for change truly exists. Before that numerical sum of 3 billion is reached, the present pattern of instability and lack of dependability, along with a population explosion, diminishes our cause through distortion or elongated struggle.

Torrential support for peace is what I request. A trickle will not help. A river is insufficient. A gigantic flood of action to spread over the entire planet is imperative, and I solicit your own efforts at once.

I say to you with the vitality of my soul, we must have 37% of humanity actually involved in stopping war and healing the planet very soon. That means each of you among the 12 to 18% we have now identified as light workers must sustain yourself and bring in two or three other dependable helpers to increase our consciousness support base. This 37% is a critical number and one that we can achieve quickly only with your help.

Though I cannot give you the full explanation of what will occur, we will add a great surprise effort when you attain 37% human support and cooperation. Believe 37% is possible! Divide 5 billion by 37% and what do you get? Approximately 1.3 billion humans. Activating that many humans can be done if you exert your soul essence to the task. There are over 1/2 billion of you now, and many more with potential.

You believe that a minority of devoted helpers can turn the tide using what you call collective consciousness, cosmic multiplication or exponential expansion. This is regrettably not quite so because of the free will factor.

Just because you are enlightened and active does not mean you can turn your positive contagion into another's practical application, though it has that potential. Sadly, on this planet, when your spirited enthusiasm passes to another human, it does not mean she or he will maintain a stable and reliable commitment in the earth/heaven marriage we seek. Many of your species who have been counted on the most have turned away, have delayed and generally proved disappointing to the plans of masters and angels alike. Most have not sustained a constant unified thought form for peace, which you must do now so that action can follow. I do not speak so frankly to cause you pain or depression, only to remind you we are dealing with energy, movement, action . . . and life. Action for positive purposes cannot be delayed.

I will repeat what I said before, for emphasis. To reach *rapid* and *permanent* change on your planet there is a need for 67% of the entire population to have one thought and intention of unified peace agreement.

The peace tempo is improving, and we acknowledge the many individuals engaged in peace activities who are already committed and are striving to do more. If you can collectively unify 37% of the population in two years, an amount that is obtainable, you have our angelic promise that a wonderful new help will be given toward the next required increment.

Help us. Help your planet. Help yourselves.

Let it be said of your human family that you awakened, you were powerfully committed, and you accomplished peace for planetary posterity.

Let this theme be your rallying thought for action, whatever words you use. PEACE FOR PLANETARY POSTERITY.

The presentation of the information in this book is for your consideration. It is a foundation to allow you to acquire a context for what is occurring beyond your physical sight and senses.

I come with this clarion call to empower your *practical solutions* to current challenges. It is given to every individual on the planet whether heard and accepted or disbelieved and denied.

Though an angel, I am not to be worshipped! for you are a concentrated beam of energy with intelligence, memory, understanding and *purpose*, even as I am. Our mutual purpose is peace and harmony throughout the universe, including your own orb. However, we are now concentrating on you, and observing all that occurs. Every aspect of your existence will be influenced or speeded up to push you into positive activities for peace. If you are frequently meditating yourself, and in a group with others, you will not lose your balance. The momentum of the Time of the Dove (within the Time of Awakening) will cause such excitement that you will not want to miss anything! A new eagerness will arise once you accept that there is no alternative to action.

About February, 1989, there will be a "breathing" space for you to accomplish tasks and utilize your unified, cooperative endeavors. This "reprieve" will last approximately four months, and all incoming information temporarily will be at a slower flow. Those who currently receive information will still continue to know, but only after the four-month period will they again disseminate the information received. Then the downpour of our expanding vibratory energy will continue. You will seem to have your "umbrella" up for awhile so the heavy rains of truth will not fall on you as you rest and consolidate individual and group efforts.

Later, the rain of change will continue. At times the sunshine may be blocked out as that rain pelts its way into your personality recognition of soul desire to preserve life. It can be likened to a flood on the surface of your physical land where rain clouds blow across a parched and arid area. At first the clouds offer coolness from the heat of the sun. There are sighs of relief. Then the actual rain starts. It *pours* on the dusty land.

Those who are thirsty run to capture the liquid one way or another. Some raise their faces so that the rain water splashes their cheeks, goes into their mouths. It travels into their throats and into their very being. It nourishes and refreshes. In such a way the waters of truth can be taken into your mind and soul so that you can begin to change. Just as the arid, parched soil changes with moisture, so too will each of you change as the waters of knowledge touch your being. Even those more advanced and spiritually aware among you will be accelerated.

You will *not* drown in this rain of energy. You will be safe. Struggles there may be, yet joy is the final intention and eventual outcome. Our positive energy comes to serve life. Humanity will gain even as flowers, plants, trees, and other growth comes forward refreshed with a new and evident vitality.

A word that soon will become very popular for each of you is *vision*. "I see" will also be used frequently. You will see with "new eyes" as the scales that have caused darkness fall away.

As the information pours on you, an important moment will come into each of your lives. In that blessed moment you will broaden your perception of reality. Truly the light will dawn. Veils will be lifted. *The God-source will be understood!* You will finally affirm that *everything relates to everything else*, especially on your planet.

As you may have learned, two magnificent rays of energy rule or operate your particular universe. These Gold and Silver Rays were created by, and are attached to, the One Source; they therefore have high creative qualities. These great beings are indescribable in their influence, and have come to change earth's negativity to harmony. You may believe that their powerful intervention is here to influence conscious awareness for all that lives.

In your technological thinking you might rank the Silver and Gold Rays as dual top management in the greatest business ever created. The president or chief would be God, of course, with the Great Rays totally in charge of the business under God. The Silver Ray has recently acquired *specific* responsibility for planet earth as support to the Gold Ray's long-term influence. During the Time of Awakening both the Gold and Silver Rays will temporarily be working together to accomplish the task of preserving all life and bringing peace on earth.

You may expect Lord Jesus and the other great religious teachers and masters, the Great Rays, and we of the angelic realm to have a unified purpose and join together for this clarion call. Follow whichever religious figure or angel you can best love and understand, yet be open to them all, if humanly possible. More than you may imagine, the greatest divine intervention for peace ever planned is now under way.

All are invited; all are included if they wish. It is our gift.

Yes, a prodigal planetary undertaking calls to your soul and personality. It sounds *now*, to recapture the wisdom, love and integrity of God's essence expressing in physical form.

How will this plan affect you? First of all, it requires your sincerity. All your thoughts and intentions will be clearly revealed in your actions. You have a saying, "Actions speak louder than words."

For those of you who do not believe in separation, let me comment thusly. Energy is real. Its qualities or nature can move from higher vibratory rates to lower, uncomfortable as this descent is. The reverse is *not true*, however. A lower or denser energy cannot rise higher without releasing negativity and those qualities related to unconsciousness. We do not say this sorting or separating must be permanent.

All will learn their own demonstration of peace and grow at whatever rate they choose. Even as water and oil are within the same container, though, their occupancy level in the container is not identical. You may not believe my example, yet please ponder how 22 electromagnetic levels may be together simultaneously, yet not be identically active in the same consciousness experience. I propose that your actions will self-select your location in that cosmic container of the 22 levels just mentioned. If separation is offensive to you as a word or concept may we suggest "placement" instead?

This information can either cause trepidation or rejoicing. All events on your planet are in a time span marked critical. Destructive circumstances may not continue. War, murder, injustices, cruelty, hunger, sorrow and whatever other negatives you may wish to list are reaching their point of saturation. Everything will be turned upside down, be shaken up, CHANGED! And then reformulated into a higher level of energy and consciousness. That is why I have been called to earth by the Silver Ray, and now I call you.

Come forward all who hear and see. Come and unite so that peace may be created on your lands. PEACE IS POSSIBLE. Let us make a long awaited vision come true!

Let that vision take root in your very essence, merge into your earth affairs, and proclaim your spiritual emancipation from violence. Regarding the galactic heritage you have spurned or forgotten, we ask that you remember it and join in a planetary confirmation of your part in earth's plan for local and galactic peace.

Now, old soul, please read the following "Call to Participate" statement that I bring to you, *silently*. Then if it has meaning for you, speak it aloud to see how it feels. Later, after reflection, if you seriously decide to answer this clarion "Call to Participate" you should enter into a quiet time of meditation, prayer, or contemplation. In this inner silence ask God (or whatever your understanding of the highest good is) to hear your affirmative answer of agreement to assist in rehabilitating the planet and protecting all life on it. If you truly speak this "Call to Participate" a third time with sincerity and purity of heart you may be sure your message will be heard and directly supported by the invisible ones who are assisting earth in this Time of Awakening.

Heartfelt commitment and willingness to consistently be caring and concerned for the planet in everyday behavior and action is what we ask you to give.

Prepare yourself for the "Call to Participate" by reading this statement.

"I look inward and see myself as a personality of good intention who affirms that a greater power than myself exists beyond this earth. I realize I do truly seek to express a growing love for life, the planet earth, and all who exist here. I accept that within myself there is a wonderful resource that can guide my choices and behaviors. Some may call it the Holy Spirit, a soul, consciousness, awareness or even common sense.

This inner guidance is something positive that I can turn to more and more by establishing quiet times in my usual daily routine. It is my choice to do this willingly and with a constant commitment, for I realize the serious need for peace and the establishment of healthy living for all humans, animals, sea life, birds, plants, and also the soil, water and air.

Having reviewed this background information about myself I stand ready to read the angelic "Call to Participate," realizing the opportunity it provides me to become a true caretaker of earth." ☞

CALL TO PARTICIPATE

I promise my personal support and allegiance to the planet where I now live and recognize that my personal peace and physical participation is greatly needed to overcome the negativity, violence and fear that have besieged this beautiful place and the majority of its inhabitants.

During the remaining years of my life I pledge my deep and consistent effort, time and concern for the healing of this planet jewel and I ask that my soul record be identified as an earth caretaker. From this day forward I accept my responsibility for, and dominion over, this planet with commitment and caring.

I give reverence to God.

_____   _____

            signed   date

Creating peace on our planet requires commitment and cooperation. If your soul has been touched or your life goals clarified by this book, perhaps you would like to share its message with friends and acquaintances . . . give copies for gifts . . . write letters to editors of newspapers, magazines, etc. about peace and preservation of life . . . seek publicity on radio and TV stations . . . plant trees . . . have a garden (even in an empty lot or along a roadway) . . . stop air, water and soil pollution through personal commitment or by joining one of the many conservation and ecology organizations.

You may wish to have a fundraising event to support such endeavors . . . form a local Love Corps group to meditate weekly . . . and generally help raise humanity's consciousness about peace and the need to preserve all life on earth.

It is vital for each of us to meditate daily and also be in a weekly meditation group (two or more persons) so that we will always have God's presence guiding our lives.

The Love Corps is an alliance of all human beings of good will who want planetary peace above everything and will work with others to achieve it.

LOVE CORPS NETWORKING

A Love Corps team frequently travels around the United States and the world to link energies, to share additional information not included in the New Teachings, Secret Truths, Cosmic Revelation and Descent of the Dove books, and to encourage humanity's achievement of peace and the preservation of all life upon planet earth. If you would like to be involved in the Love Corps endeavors, to participate with us in seminars, or to have an individual soul reading, please write for information so we can possibly include your area in our itinerary.

This Time of Awakening brings new information in a flow, or a spiral, to move each of us to a higher level of achievement and involvement. You are encouraged to accept the responsibility of this and immediately unite efforts with other people in creating peaceful attitudes and conditions on our planet.

PARTICIPATION QUESTIONNAIRE
AND ORDER FORM

To: SPIRITUAL EDUCATION ENDEAVORS (S.E.E.)*
        1556 Halford Avenue, #288
        Santa Clara, CA 95051 USA

Having read <u>Descent of the Dove</u>, I want to participate in spreading its message. The way I choose to do this is indicated below.

Here's my gift to support and/or expand the **LOVE CORPS** efforts.
_____ $1,000 or more___ $500___ $250___ $100 Other $ _____
(For tax-deductible contribution, make check payable to The Share Foundation*)

I wish to donate my skills and/or time for: _____ Secretarial/Clerical
_____ Fundraising _____ Graphic Arts _____ Word Processing
_____ Bookkeeping & Accounting _____ Public Speaking
_____ Translating _____ Publicity _____ Promotion/Publication
_____ Other (specify): _____

I have the following equipment and technical know-how:
_____ Personal Computer: Make/Model _____
_____ CB Radio _____ Ham radio equipment

Please send information on how I can help disseminate <u>Descent of the Dove</u> to:
_____ Friends, Bookstores Churches, and Organizations
_____ Other countries

I would like to help publicize <u>Descent of the Dove</u>:
_____ On Radio _____ On T.V. _____ In Newspapers/Magazines
_____ Other (specify): _____

I would like to be a networker or contact person for the **LOVE CORPS** in my area. _____

Check if holding a meditation group others may attend. _____
May we give others your address and telephone number? _____

*The Share Foundation (Fed. EIN 94-2699567)

(Continued on reverse)

Please send me the **Love Corps** Newsletter:
_____ A 12 month subscription for 1988 is $24, $_____
or $2 per issue. Circle month(s) desired:

J F M A M J J A S O N D $_____

_____ Foreign 1988 12 month subscription is $36
airmail, single issues $3 each, U.S. Dollars only. $_____

_____ 1989 Bi-monthly is $18. $_____

_____ 1989 Foreign bi-monthly is $30,
U.S. Dollars only. $_____

Please send me additional copies of:
Descent of the Dove:
        Quantity _____ @$9.95 per copy $_____

I wish to order _____ copies of New Teachings
for an Awakening Humanity @ $8.95 per copy $_____

I wish to order _____ copies of Secret Truths
for Teens & Twenties @ $7.95 per copy $_____

I wish to order _____ copies of Cosmic
Revelation @ $9.95 per copy $_____

Minus discount if applicable (see below)** $_____
Plus 6.5% sales tax (CA residents only) $_____
Plus shipping for 1 book (in U.S. only)*** $_____1.80_____
Plus $.80 shipping for each additional book
to the same address $_____

        Total for books $_____

TOTAL ENCLOSED $_____

Please Print
Name _____

Address _____

City/State/Zip _____

Phone (optional) (___) _____

Love Corps Volunteer discounts:
        5-9 books @ 10% off plus shipping
        10 or more books @ 20% off plus shipping
***Please request foreign shipping rates.

NOTES

NOTES

NOTES